PHILOSOPHY OF SILVER BIRCH

PHILOSOPHY OF SILVER BIRCH

Edited by
STELLA STORM

The Spiritual Truth Press

First published 1969
Seventh impression 2004
This impression 2012

The Spiritual Truth Press
15 Broom Hall, Oxshott
Surrey KT22 OJZ

ISBN 978 0 85384 103 6

Printed in Great Britain by Booksprint

INTRODUCTION

There are a number of possible reasons why you are reading this book. The first and most likely is that you are already a 'follower' of Silver Birch and have found his great wisdom and spiritual insights of benefit in your life. In this case you will welcome this reprint of one of the classic books of his teachings. Maybe you have been given this book by a friend who believes its message of love, in this world and the next, will inspire or comfort you. If so, you will not be disappointed.

Perhaps you chanced upon it on a bookshelf or saw it advertised, then curiosity got the better of you. Well, after reading its pages you may also decide that 'chance' played no part in the decision and that some form of spiritual guidance has brought you and this book together.

Whatever the reason, the chances are that Silver Birch's wisdom will remain with you forever. Long after you have forgotten his precise words, his guidance will still be a very real influence whenever you need it. And if you need to jog your memory just reach for this book and read it again. Silver Birch's words are so accessible and meaningful that you will never tire of reading them. But who is Silver Birch, the spirit guide whose words are faithfully recorded here? And who was Murices Bearable, the London medium who channelled that wisdom? Without an answer to these questions, many new readers – however impressed with these teachings – will be puzzled about their source.

Barbanell was the founder and editor of a weekly Spiritualist newspaper, Psychic News, and for half a century devoted his life to spreading spiritual knowledge through its columns and those of other publications with which he was associated. In his own obituary, which he wrote before his passing at the age of 79 on July 17th 1981, he revealed that he was told by Estelle Roberts' Red Cloud – a spirit guide for whom he had the greatest admiration – that in a previous incarnation he had made a promise to reincarnate and devote his life to spreading Spiritualism. Though he had no knowledge of that life or promise, events certainly conspired to make it possible.

He was born to Jewish parents in a poor area of London's East End. His mother was devoutly religious but his father, a barber, was an atheist so Barbanell heard many arguments about religion during his early years. His father always won, and his son adopted the same outlook but later changed to agnosticism. Yet after hearing about Spiritualism from a speaker at a social and literary club of which he was secretary, Barbanell refused to start the debate by putting an opposing view – one of his duties – because, he explained, he had made no personal investigation and therefore his opinions were valueless. This impressed the speaker who invited Barbanell to attend a seance in which a medium, Mrs Blaustein, was entranced by various spirits of different nationalities. He was not impressed, and on a second visit fell asleep. Barbanell apologised, believing that either boredom or tiredness had been responsible, but the other circle members informed him that he had not been asleep but had been in trance and a Red Indian had spoken through him.

With the enccouragement of famous Fleet Street journalist Hannen Swaffer, Barbanell founded *Psychic News* partly as a vehicle for the guide's teachings. But, because he knew he would be criticised for publishing his own mediumship in his own newspaper, Barbanell did not reveal to his readers for many years who was channelling the wisdom, by which time the guide had a huge following on his own merits.

Silver Birch spoke regularly at Barbanell's home circle and the proceedings were always recorded in shorthand.

There were a number of differences in style and procedure between Barbanell's own journalistic efforts and the way in which Silver Birch communicated, as Barbanell himself observed:

"In my working life I use words every day. I have never yet written or dictated an article with which I was satisfied when I read it. Inevitably I find, when looking at the typed material, that I can improve it by altering words, phrases and sentences. No such problem arises with the guide's teachings. These flow perfectly, requiring usually only punctuation. Another interesting aspect is the occasional use of words that I regard as archaic and do not form part of my normal vocabulary."

But who was Silver Birch? A psychic artist depicts him as a serious-looking native American Indian with a single feather and compassionate eyes. There is evidence to suggest that this was simply a convenient persona behind which a far more spiritually-evolved soul hid in order that those who read his words would judge them not by the name attached to them but by the wisdom that pervades every sentence.

Those of us who knew them both were well aware of the differences in the way they spoke and the words they used. They both had spiritual missions and they fulfilled them admirably, particularly when working together in their unique two-world partnership. This, as you are about to discover, has provided us with simple, uplifting, comforting and inspirational answers to the questions we all ask, from time to time, about life and its purpose. They are needed now more than ever before as we prepare for the challenges that will confront us in the 21st century.

Roy Stemman
Chairman
Spiritual Truth Foundation

CONTENTS

SILVER BIRCH by Sylvia Barbanell   10

FOREWORD   11

1. WHY DID SILVER BIRCH RETURN?   25
2. THE RESULT OF HIS MISSION   33
3. THE ALL-PERVADING POWER OF THE SPIRIT   41
4. THE INESCAPABLE NATURAL LAW   45
5. LESSONS OF BEREAVEMENT   49
6. THE RESPONSIBILITY OF MEDIUMSHIP   55
7. HEALING, THE GREATEST GIFT OF ALL   67
8. RELIGION – AS SEEN BY SILVER BIRCH   81
9. IF SILVER BIRCH APPEARED ON TELEVISION   87
10. YOUTH QUESTIONS SILVER BIRCH   91
11. ASPECTS OF ANIMAL SURVIVAL   101
12. OUTSIDE THE CIRCLE   111
13. SILVER BIRCH SUMS UP   141
14. SELECTED SILVER BIRCH SAYINGS   145

"Philosophy: A mainstream of thought concerned with 'Deism,' the doctrine of a rational world, ruled over by an impersonal God, 'the first great cause'."

Concise Oxford Dictionary of English Literature

SILVER BIRCH

Though we have never met on earthly plane
He is my friend, my counsellor and guide,
My strength and comfort in the days of pain,
The unseen presence constant by my side.

He understands life's problems and its needs,
(By facing trials does noble status grow!)
He points the way of conduct in all deeds,
Knowing we do but reap the seeds we sow.

In words of simple wisdom he will say
That service is the spirit's only coin,
The paths of love and kindness lead the way
To the true Source wherein all roads conjoin.

SYLVIA BARBANELL

FOREWORD

Silver Birch's teachings have been produced through a human instrument too often aware of his failings and weaknesses. Through the years I have learned to love and respect this saintly guide whom I have never seen.

MAURICE BARBANELL

Silver Birch has an aura of majesty. He is a very great soul who comes in the guise of an Indian.

LILIAN BAILEY, the famous medium, who has clairvoyantly seen Silver Birch many times.

We sat, a round dozen, fanned circle-wise. Casually chatting, I found it difficult to concentrate on my neighbour's conversation. My eyes were fixed on the small, dapper man sitting in the right-hand corner of the sofa. Under the hypnotic drone of many voices, I watched his transformation. An articulate conversationalist, he became still, withdrawing from the desultory discussion.

Removing his thick, horn-rimmed spectacles and wrist watch, he lowered his head, rubbed his eyes and clasped his hands between his knees. His chin rested on his chest as if he had dozed off.

In a few minutes the physical body I know so well took on a new dimension. With shoulders hunched, he slowly raised his head. Although my companions seemed oblivious, quietly talking among themselves, they were obviously aware of our host's departure. A sudden deferential silence descended as our guest of honour addressed us.

My down-to-earth chief, Maurice Barbanell, had temporarily left us. Silver Birch, his well-loved guide, had "borrowed" his body and was in our midst. In slow, slightly guttural tones, quite unlike his fast-talking medium, he greeted us affectionately and embarked on his customary opening invocation, couched in unsurpassed prose:

'Oh Great White Spirit, Thou who has created us in Thy divine image and endowed us with a portion of Thy divinity, we strive to draw close and strengthen the unity that exists between Thee and us and one another.

'For all that we have received, for all the wisdom that has been vouchsafed us, for all the assurance of the infinite purpose as it has been revealed to us, we express our gratitude and pray that we may be worthy to receive even greater understanding.

'For too long we have seen through a glass darkly, misinterpreted Thee and Thy purpose, not und Thee as Thou art to us.erstanding our place in Thy infinite scheme. But now we know that we have the inestimable privilege of participating in the processes of eternal creation.

'It is Thy love which has guided us all into this knowledge and given us a more comprehensive picture of Thee, of ourselves and of the wondrous universe in which we are placed.

'We know that we are for ever united with Thee, that there is nothing at any time on earth or in the spheres beyond that can sever this divine bond that exists. Always, therefore, we are within Thy ken and care, always we are subject to Thy providence, always we are accessible to

'Some of us have been privileged to be the bearers of that power of the spirit which brings such beneficence in its train, guiding, comforting, upholding, healing and pointing the way for many who thought they were for ever lost.

'We express our gratitude for all the labours of the many pioneers on both sides of the veil, for all who have striven to break down the obstacles and barriers, and for all who still labour to ensure a fuller and more complete descent of the power of the spirit.

'May all that is said and done be in keeping with what has been made manifest to us. And may we, before we close, realise that we have been taken another step on the road of understanding that always leads to Thee.

'This is the prayer of Thy Indian servant who seeks to serve.'

It was my first visit to what must be the most famous home circle. Held in Barbanell's flat, it is still called the Hannen Swaffer home circle in our greatest propagandist's honour, though he has emigrated to the Other Side.

My editor, as inseparable from the inevitable cigar as Churchill, was now standing somewhere in the wings playing the unusual part of understudy. The leading role had been taken over by one of the most renowned North American Indian guides in two worlds. The personality change was striking. Silver Birch gives the impression of a wise old soul. Barbanell seems to shrivel slightly inside his immaculate suit and become elderly.

I find it difficult to identify the guide with Marcel Poncin's psychic portrait of him hanging on the sitting-room wall. This portrays Silver Birch as a young, strong, upright Indian chief. When controlling Barbanell, he manifests as a venerable patriarch.

Poncin, famous as a French artist and actor, was not clairvoyant. His psychic faculty operated through his own medium of painting. He produced Silver Birch's likeness without a sitter, inspired, working feverishly in half-light.

The accuracy of its resemblance to the guide has been confirmed by several mediums. This, and many other guides' portraits by Poncin, were executed at great speed, in a style totally different from his normal art work.

Poncin, who passed on fifteen years ago, must have been thrilled to meet, in the spirit world, the original models whose features he knew only from his own canvases.

*   *   *

The Silver Birch-Barbanell two-worlds partnership was, without doubt, the best-kept secret of the British psychic scene. When, in the 1930s, reports of Silver Birch's communications began to appear in print, their impact was tremendous. His simple eloquence adapts perfectly to the written word,

"Rarely has the English language been so gently, simply and so beautifully used," said one journalist. After reading the first book of Silver Birch's teachings, Lord Beaverbrook wrote: "It contains passages of great beauty. I was struck by the simplicity of the work."

Barbanell, a professional writer, editor and journalist, has manipulated words for most of his working life. He has paid tribute to his guide, "who delivers spontaneously utterances of such purity that they glisten like diamonds. I salute a master of English, a great literary craftsman," he said.

It was another famous Spiritualist, who also lived by his pen, who recognised from the start that the guide's teachings should be published. Hannen Swaffer decided they were not given to the home circle for private use but must be broadcast.

Barbanell agreed on one condition. He was the editor of a Spiritualist newspaper. "If I reveal I am the medium there could be criticism that publication flatters my vanity," he said. "I will leave my name out and let Silver Birch's teachings stand or fall on their own merit."

Realising he could be accused of self-publicity if he were identified with Silver Birch, he felt subsequent denigration might diminish the guide's great personal qualities. The wisdom of his decision has been amply proved. For a score of years the guide's philosophy stood tall on its own merit.

As Swaffer wrote : "Silver Birch now has more followers than any earthly preacher. They belong to every clime and almost every race and are people of all shades of colour."

* * *

The circle called the guide by an affectionate nickname which they did not wish to appear in print. When the decision was made to publish his teachings, they asked him to choose a more suitable pseudonym. He selected "Silver Birch." The next morning Barbanell found on his desk an anonymous postcard from a Scottish reader. It was a photograph of silver birch trees!

Over the years, circle visitors were asked to respect the anonymity of Silver Birch's medium. Despite the many rumours, it is greatly to their credit that they were not confirmed until Barbanell himself chose to release the longawaited information.

When I asked a close friend, related to an original circle member, to tell me in strict confidence who was the medium, she honoured the code, declining to confirm or deny the gossip. The psychic grapevine had given signals that Swaffer, Sylvia Barbanell, his wife, and even Barbanell himself was the medium.

As Barbanell seemed the most unlikely channel for a spirit guide, I rejected the suggestion. A shrewd, working journalist, though his whole adult life has been geared to propagating Spiritualism, he seemed the antithesis of a medium. A dedicated Spiritualist of many years' experience and a fine platform exponent, he was out of character with the gentle spirit philosopher.

Barbanell's ample contribution to the Movement through his pen, editorship of two leading psychic journals, a dozen books and his nation-wide propaganda meetings, led to his title of "Mr. Spiritualism." To think he could also be the medium for one of the best-loved and most widely-read guides was, I thought, too much. Silver Birch is an eloquent teacher; Barbanell a fighting rebel.

I well remember his dramatic revelation in Two Worlds ten years ago. With typical economy of words he wrote: "The time has come to make public what has for long been a 'secret.' Who is Silver Birch's medium? The answer is – "I am." A surge of "There, I told you so," went through the Spiritualist ranks.

To disprove the "secondary personality" theory it has often been pointed out that Barbanell disagreed with his guide's support of reincarnation. In many public debates on this subject, Barbanell usually won. But, after following Silver Birch's teachings, he admits that his opinion has gradually changed. "Now I am prepared to believe that, in exceptional circumstances, individuals voluntarily reincarnate for a special task," he says.

Silver Birch has great breadth of wisdom and humanity. He never criticises, finds fault or blames individuals. On the other hand, Barbanell admits to being highly critical and sometimes impatient. Apart from the guide's uniquely individual manner, one can only truly appreciate the "separateness" of these two men if you have met Silver Birch "in the flesh," and worked closely with Barbanell, as I have done. The difference is distinct.

*   *   *

I have shared Barbanell's professional life for some years, first as editorial secretary and now as a reporter. Very occasionally I have been conscious of Silver Birch slightly overshadowing him – when he dictated a Two Worlds editorial, for instance. I once commented on this, but he curtly dismissed the suggestion. I think I'm right, though.

Normally his dictation concerns topics and news items on Spiritualism. Though articulate, he pauses and alters sentences. Then comes editing before he is satisfied with the final result. On the now rare occasions when he speaks publicly, he naturally relies on notes.

Gazing out of the window, however, he can dictate, without hesitation, a perfectly composed leading article on an "ideas" theme as though inspired. The words flow without interruption in the same fashion as Silver Birch. Editing is unnecessary. But there the similarity ends.

A man is acknowledged by his style, particularly in writing. Silver Birch's style, wholly consistent and easily recognisable, bears no resemblance to that of his medium.

Barbanell needs no preparation before going into trance. I once suggested he should have a few minutes' rest or quiet meditation in his office before driving home. He prefers to work till the last moment with no "withdrawal" from his busy normal life. And the circle is always held on a Friday evening, the last day of his strenuous week.

He goes straight from the hurly-burly and stress of a bustling newspaper office. On the few occasions I have attended the circle, Barbanell has driven me to his flat. I snuggled into the back seat, determined not to talk shop or chatter, leaving him in peace to "tune in" to the coming séance. The short car journey needs no concentration. He could probably do it blindfolded!

He was the piper who called the tune, discussing the day's office events, chatting naturally on general and psychic subjects – usually our main topic because, though our life is spent with them, we still find them completely engrossing. In fact, he was his normal gregarious self, with no indication of impending deep trance.

Only when he settles in his accustomed couch corner does he relax, preparing to change places with his spirit guardian. I couldn't help comparing this well-adjusted, two-worlds exchange with the theatrical preliminaries – and finales – of some mediums who make a production of their séances.

I am being critical and intolerant. As Silver Birch has rightly said: "Every form of communication depends on the use of a human instrument. Wherever you have the human instrument, that communication must be tinged by the channel through which it operates, because being a human channel, it cannot be devoid of its own nature."

Coming out of trance, Barbanell shows no sign of weariness. After wiping his eyes and replacing his spectacles and watch he has a drink of water. In a few seconds he joins animatedly in general conversation with his friends and guests over a vegetarian buffet refreshment. By common consent Silver Birch's talk is seldom discussed.

*　　*　　*

This famous home circle has six regular sitters besides the medium. Sylvia Barbanell, naturally the veteran attendant, has said: "I have heard Silver Birch speak through the lips of his entranced medium many hundreds of times, yet I do not recall an occasion when I have ever been bored by his words."

Similar comments come from the other five loyal Silver Birch circle attendants. Probably the most important member is the stenographer, Frances Moore, who for over thirty years has faithfully recorded the guide's utterances.

On occasions, tape recorders have failed, but Frances' perfectly typed transcripts arrive on Barbanell's desk regularly after each sitting. These form the basis of the Two Worlds' reports of the guide's teachings.

Frances, a gentle self-effacing woman with a sweet disposition, is always accompanied by her husband, Vernon. An ex-Methodist missionary, now an executive with an internationally famous company, Vernon is an articulate debater and still contributes many thought-provoking questions to Silver Birch.

This couple were "spiritually" married by Silver Birch thirty years ago, at a Hannen Swaffer home circle. The sitting was prior to their forthcoming church wedding. The guide's views on marriage are worth recording here: "I want you to realise that you begin now the greatest adventure of all, for two lives that have pursued separate courses are now come together to begin a united life. Soon a "man of God" will read a few words from a book and, according to your world of matter, you will be joined in the bonds of holy matrimony.

But I say to you there are no bonds unless you bind one another with love and affection. There are no ties unless you wish to tie one another with love and affection.

Remember that you are two spiritual beings, both portions of the Great Spirit, now coming together with pledges to cherish, to love and to serve one another even as a great' love from this world strives to serve you both.

Do not expect that you will escape occasional sadness and sorrow, difficulty, trial and test, for these are parts of your evolution. When they arise, as arise they inevitably must, face them with honesty and know that they help to quicken your character and bring you closer together.

There are many here who look forward with joy to a celebration which will duplicate the one you have in your church, but which will be sanctified in our world by ties we regard as more enduring, for the promises uttered audibly by word of mouth are as nothing compared with the unspoken pledges of the soul.

You are richly blessed, for you have knowledge. I wish you, on behalf of many here who stand beside me, a safe journey through life's seas, happiness and joy abounding, but always ask you to remember that you continue to serve with the added fortification of love around you in the earthly world.

*   *   *

The other three circle members are Nettie Abrahams and George and Rene Jessup, who, between them, clock up practically the same long attendance as the Moores. Despite their familiarity with Silver Birch's teaching over these long years, they are dedicated followers of his philosophy.

Jessup, a well-known healer with many successes to his credit, spoke enthusiastically to me of Silver Birch the last time I visited the home circle. He is always finding fresh truth emerging each time he listens to the guide. His bedside reading is one of the Silver Birch books, which, he says, gives an added dimension to his simple eloquence.

Nettie, a steadfast tolerant woman, has grown in spiritual stature through many family setbacks and sorrows. She says but for Silver Birch's wise counsel, she could not have conquered ill-health and several bereavements.

This harmonious group are certainly a great credit to their well-loved guide and mentor.

*   *   *

I am your friend and will always be at your side. I have a large family and try to help every member of it. When you go away from here this night you will not go away empty-handed. A part of the power of the spirit, the most precious, force in the universe, will go with you to remain with you all the time.

SILVER BIRCH

*   *   *

The dearest wish of many Spiritualists is an invitation (they are extended by the guide) to attend this famous home circle. In the past this was naturally sometimes prompted by curiosity about the medium's identity. I must confess it was so in my case.

I have known the Barbanells for thirty years, but my first confrontation with Silver Birch was only seven years ago. My husband and widowed mother were invited with me. We were fascinated by the transformation. My quicksilver chief became a gentle being, working on a much slower vibration.

With typical tender understanding, Silver Birch made a magnificent gesture on Mother's behalf. Realising she had difficulty following him, due to her deafness, he asked her to sit beside him on the couch. Normally this select position is occupied by Barbanell's wife, Sylvia. Silver Birch suggested they changed places.

My mother referred to my young sister's tragic passing, which led us to investigate Spiritualism. The guide commented: "Through the greatest sorrow you get the greatest knowledge. The soul learns its lessons in the hour of seeming darkness. It comes into its own, not when the sun is shining, the birds are singing and all is bright.

"It is in the darkness, in difficulty, doubt and despair, in sorrow and sickness that the soul finds itself. When you are able to make a true assessment you will find that it was a necessary prelude to bring you spiritual understanding."

"But you feel very rebellious when a loved one is taken," she countered.

"Mental rebellion is not bad, it is a good discipline. It never harms the soul to question. The mind should be stimulated to search. If it rebels it is a stimulus to find out more. The Great Spirit has so equipped you potentially that you should be able to face and conquer every experience that comes your way. No circumstance is your master.

"By virtue of your latent divinity, which is a repository of potential, infinite strength, you have the power to rise above all that earthly life can bring. If you allow yourself to be brought down by the storm, you have not learned the lesson that the storm has to offer. You should be able to rise above it.

"Withdraw for a while, ask questions when you have doubts. Again and again go over the basis of your belief and see if it will stand the test. When you find that it does, you are the better for it. When you find that it does not, then change your outlook, for there is still more truth for you to acquire. Is that not reasonable?"

*   *   *

"Reasonable" is probably the best description of Silver Birch's philosophy. I quote his own words:

"There is nothing that appeals more to an old soul like myself than to see you testing everything at the bar of reason. We enthrone reason as the great guide. Always reject what your reason rejects, no matter through whom it comes or the source. These are the truths that should appeal to reason and intelligence. If reason revolts and intelligence is insulted, then discard them."

*   *   *

For the sake of those many thousands who love Silver Birch, follow his guidance and try to put his principles into practice-but who are unlikely ever to meet him in this world-I have tried to fill in the background of the guide, his medium and the circle. For over thirty years Silver Birch's teachings have appeared regularly, first in *Psychic News*, the weekly newspaper, and latterly in *Two Worlds*, the monthly psychic magazine, both edited by Barbanell. Eight best-selling books have been published, many being translated into several languages. It is impossible to measure Silver Birch's world-wide influence.

This book is my attempt at a definitive study, a composite portrait, of this beloved spirit sage, based on his perennial philosophy.

STELLA STORM

I know that you have been reading words I have spoken in days gone by. I hope that I live up to them, because with great skill they have depicted me as a wise old man. I sometimes fail to recognise myself in that description.

SILVER BIRCH

Chapter One

WHY DID SILVER BIRCH RETURN?

I did not want to come back to your world. It has very little to attract once you have passed beyond its vibrations. The realm or sphere which is my natural habitat has a radiance and translucence that you cannot understand, clogged as you are by matter.

Your world seemed unattractive, but there was a job to be done. I was told it would be difficult. I had to learn the language, I had to find my friends and had to earn their love. I had to find a means of ensuring that the mouthpiece I use should convey the fundamental truths of the spirit and reach as many as possible. I was assured that all help would be given if I played my part. And so it has all come to pass.

SILVER BIRCH

I was asked, many long years ago, whether I would return to the world of matter and find on earth a band who would work with me to deliver the message of the spirit. I was told I would have to find an instrument so that I would be able to express through him the message I was charged to deliver. So I searched our records and found my medium. I watched from the time he was conceived and from the moment the spirit began to express itself. I brought my influence to bear and started there and then this association which has lasted all these years.

I helped to mould the spirit and the tiny little mind. Throughout every phase of his life I watched every experience, learned how to associate closely with him and accustomed myself through his boyhood days to all the mental processes and physical habits. I studied my instrument from every aspect – mind, spirit and physical body.

Then I had to guide his footsteps towards an understanding of these spirit truths. First, I led him to make a study of the many religions in your world of matter, until his mind revolted and he became, what you call, an atheist. Now he was ready for me to begin my task of speaking through his lips.

I guided him to his first meeting. I led him to his first circle. There, in the power provided, I made my first contact – so crude, so trivial, but from my point of view, so important – and uttered my first expression in the world of matter through another's organism.

From that day I learned how to obtain better control until now you see the result. We have achieved so much that I can register the totality of my ideas and eliminate for all purposes what is in the medium's own personality.

When I undertook my mission I was told: "You will have to go into the world of matter and, when you have found your instrument, you will have to bring to him sympathetic souls who will aid you to deliver your message." I searched, found you all and brought you together.

The greatest difficulty I had to face was the choice whether I would return to provide those proofs that your world must have to satisfy itself – material proofs, I mean, not spiritual ones – or whether I would return as a teacher of truth. I chose the harder.

With the manifold experiences I had had in the spirit realms, I decided to appeal to the judgment of mature, evolved minds. I would reveal the message of the spirit in all its simplicity. I would strive to manifest love, never to reproach with anger, and prove by precept and example that I was what I claimed to be – a messenger of the Great Spirit.

I imposed upon myself the burden of anonymity, so that I would make no appeal of illustrious personage, title, rank or fame, but would be judged on what I said.

I am a voice crying in the wilderness. I am a servant of the Great Spirit. What does it matter who I am? Judge me by what I strive to do. If my words, earnestness, determination, my mission among you, bring comfort or light to one who is struggling in darkness, then I am happy.

Your world has for too long concerned itself with teachers whom it has aggrandised into exaggerated positions and has forgotten what they came to teach. Our mission is not to exalt men and women into high places of authority, but to seek to reveal truth, knowledge and wisdom. What does it matter whether I am a teacher of great distinction or a lowly beggar, so long as the seal of truth stamps what I say?

We preach nothing that is untrue, undignified, ignoble or debases mankind. We seek to reveal only that which will elevate the whole human race and give it a true conception of its position in life and the universe, its relationship to the Great Spirit and an understanding of its kinship with other members of the vast human family in your world.

They are not new ideas we try to teach you. They are the old, old truths that those who see with the eyes of the spirit have taught for many years. But you have neglected them and so it is necessary for us to teach them to you once again, to show you that you must learn the lessons of the Great Spirit.

You have nearly destroyed your world by the follies of your ideas. There is war that need not be, for if you knew these truths, and lived them, men would not kill. There is starvation when there is plenty of the Great Spirit's bounty. There are mean hovels where the children of the Great Spirit are compelled to live, deprived of fresh air, unable to catch the health-giving rays of the sun, forced to live below the line of sustenance. There are want, distress and misery.

Throughout the whole world of matter there is a great cloud of discontent. There *will* come the Spring of dreams and the Summer of fulfilment. It will come quickly or slowly as the children of the Great Spirit exercise their free will.

Wherever one man strives to uplift another, behind him there are a thousand spirits who try to make his victory a greater one. No effort for good can ever be lost. No desire to serve can ever be wasted. There must be a pioneer who hacks his way through the forest and makes the path a little easier for those who follow. Gradually this path is beaten down and worn smooth.

Sometimes I see the many masters in my world, with tears in their eyes, looking down on the follies of those who, one day, will realise how they have thrown away their great opportunities of raising up the children of earth. And sometimes I see their faces wreathed in smiles because some unknown man has rendered a service which lights a new torch of hope in the world.

Like many others, I have come nearer to the earth vibrations to help push forward that great new world which waits just round the corner. I come to teach you the laws of the Great Spirit and to show you how, if you live according to them, the bounty of the Great Spirit can be poured into your hearts and minds.

It is always with a sense of flatness that I return to your world. It is void of light and life. It is dull, drab and lacks vitality. It is like an old cushion in which the spring has gone and everything sags. An atmosphere of gloom hangs everywhere. So very few are filled with the joy of life; despair and indifference are on every hand.

I come from a realm where all is light and colour, where hearts sing with the sheer joy of living, where all are busily engaged in congenial pursuits, where all the arts flourish, where each is imbued with the idea of service, with sharing what he has with those who have it not, where there is an intensity and vitality, a joy and radiance in well-doing.

Here I see only a world filled with sorrow that should be full of happiness, darkness where there should be light, hunger where there should be plenty. The Great Spirit has provided everything and yet there are those who prevent its distribution. There are obstacles which must be swept away.

I cannot do it. I can only tell you how the Law can work if you, who are still encased in matter, will allow it to work through you. Show in your own lives that you know the things of the spirit because the power of the spirit is in you.

If I can teach you the laws and how they work, then I rejoice. If, between us, we can bring happiness where there was unhappiness, knowledge where there was ignorance, then at least we shall have done some service. We do not seek to take away from you the responsibilities of your own lives, but only to try to inspire you to live so that men may know the Great Spirit is working through you.

* * *

It is the same old guide with the same old message, the same old truth, trying to preach it – not to the same old world, for the world is changing and more and more are beginning to hearken to the voice of wisdom and become receptive to the power of the spirit.

This truth has made great progress. I wish you could see the extent of our influence. I am proud that because of our efforts we have accomplished so much. Hearts that were once sad are now a little more joyful. Light has pierced the gloom of darkness. There is a little more knowledge where before there was ignorance.

I am not given to vaunting. The more I see of the universe, the more I am filled with true humility. Yet I know of the power to guide you. It is given to souls like myself, not because we are what we are, but because of what we seek to do. The guidance has been freely given throughout the years of our association; that guidance will continue as long as you desire it.

I must remind you that I am only an instrument, one of many seeking to bring you the truth, the simple truth of the spirit, the realisation that you are all parts of the Great Spirit of all life.

You have a divine heritage and are entitled to all the bounty of the Great Spirit because of your latent divinity. All obstacles and institutions that stand in the way of that fullness must be swept aside. Our labour is not only to free the souls and minds but the bodies also.

That is the task to which we have dedicated ourselves. That is the service we strive to perform. If I, as an instrument am privileged to bring you those truths which help you, then I rejoice.

I have worked among you for some time and will continue, so that through our united efforts we may bring some badly needed help into your world. You have the knowledge, the truth, the responsibility that comes with all knowledge of using it so that you are greater instruments.

Think not of me as just a voice that speaks to you for a few moments, but as a living, pulsating presence that is always round and about you, seeking to bring you whatever is best for your unfoldment and evolution.

I have striven to serve you, to bring you closer together in bonds of love. I have tried to teach you the laws of a higher realm, a greater life, how wondrously you are fashioned.

I have tried to show you your own responsibilities of using truth in service. I have taught you to look beyond the formalism of religious ceremony, so that you can get at the real kernel of all religion, giving service to those who need it.

In a world full of despair, weariness, doubt and difficulty, I have endeavoured to reveal those truths which will help you to help others to find the precious knowledge which spells happiness to all humanity.

If shadows cross your path, if troubles lie upon you, if doubt stirs your mind and perplexity finds a dwelling place within you, remember they are not realities. Give them wings and send them speedily forth on their flight.

Remember the mighty force that set the whole universe in motion and created every manifestation of life, both animate and inanimate; that fashioned the stars and the planets, the sun and the moon; that brought life to your world of matter; that gave your consciousness a portion of the divine spirit; that is revealed in the perfect laws that control every phase of manifestation.

That power cannot fail you if you do not fail it. Let that be your strength, your refuge and your harbour. Know that the cloak of divine love is always about you and the infinite embrace holds you in its arms.

There is no one like him in literature. Discerning readers recognise his inspiration is from a source divine and spiritual. The simplicity of his language is at times teasingly profound. One has to pause in admiration and joy when the inner meaning is gleaned.

A READER'S TRIBUTE

Chapter Two

THE RESULT OF HIS MISSION

The printed word has great potency. The speech is forgotten, the picture that flickers on your little screen is very ephemeral and the words that come with it do not make an indelible impression. But the printed word endures. It is therefor reference. It can be seen and its implications considered again and again. It can be passed round from one to another, across oceans to reach perhaps those living alone in isolation. These teachings which I express because I am fortunate enough to have access to this wisdom, become, through the medium of the stenographer, the printed word. Thus here and there a soul is touched, the seed does bear fruit.

SILVER BIRCH

There, in Silver Birch's own words, is the answer to why he chose the mission of teacher and picked Barbanell as his medium. He was addressing a fellow-craftsman, who uses his pen – or rather, typewriter – to spread spiritual truths. Brother John, *Psychic News'* well-loved and prolific columnist, was paying his first visit to the Hannen Swaffer home circle.

For twenty years, without missing an issue, John has accomplished the phenomenal feat of a regular weekly article for *Psychic News*, propounding his sound ideas, always having something fresh to say.

His contributions number over a thousand. As an added labour of love he personally answers his huge postbag. During 1967 he received, and replied to, over 1,400 letters asking for help and advice and commenting on his column. In his own gentle, modest way, like Silver Birch he never wearies of disseminating the proven fact of personal survival after death and its far-reaching implications. His medium is also the printed word.

Two previous editors of Silver Birch books have said that cold print cannot do justice to the guide's warm humanity and the love that emanates from him. Of course they are right. Those who share the privilege of meeting Silver Birch have indeed experienced a unique and moving two-worlds relationship.

Though my personal meetings with Silver Birch have been infrequent, I disagree that his personal manifestation is the most important facet of his character and the main purpose of his chosen task. Impressive at source, when I read the transcripts of the sittings I attended, the written word had a two-fold impact.

Researching for this book, I was amazed at the potency of his message, the alchemy with which he constructs every telling phrase and sentence – with no thought or preparation. I have read all the Silver Birch books. One of my tasks is proof-reading his monthly *Two Worlds* contribution.

Yet when I came to edit extracts for this latest book, I had no sense of repetition or boredom. Though it is "the same old guide with the same old message," re-reading his counsel, the innate truth and simplicity are fresh and evergreen. You cannot question its durability.

Swaffer, after fifteen years, was able to write, "I have listened for an hour or more at a time to his teachings, his guidance and his counsel and learned to love and respect him more than I love and respect any earthly being."

Through the wonderful electronic device of tape recordings, it is now possible for his followers in many lands to listen to his voice. But surely the written transcriptions of his consistently compassionate communications are the very essence of his self-appointed task.

The true value of his philosophy is measured by its world-wide influence on people who can never hope to meet him in person on this plane.

As he says, he had to find a mouthpiece who could convey the fundamental spirit truths to as many people as possible. It explains his choice of Barbanell, who, as editor of two Spiritualist publications, has the means at his disposal of circulating Silver Birch's teachings far and wide.

* * *

"My Silver Birch sitting was the most wonderful experience for many a day," wrote Brother John. "What he said to me brought tears to my eyes. I felt a great sense of attunement with him which affected me emotionally... It was an unforgettable evening."

Here are extracts from that sitting.

'I am very glad to have you here, son. I have to warn you that a very exaggerated picture is painted of me, and I do not possess all this great wisdom that seems to be attributed to me. I am only a human being like yourself, subject to weakness and imperfections and mistakes. But I have a little knowledge about spiritual things, and I will share them with any who will accept them.

They are not mine, I am only the mouthpiece. I was asked to perform this service and I will continue until the time comes for me to withdraw because the task is accomplished. That is not yet, there is still some time to go. Much has been accomplished and there is still more to be done.

The power of the spirit can sometimes perform wonders when the conditions are right, when there is no fear, when there is faith founded on knowledge, confidence born of experience.

Son, you are where you are because of the power of the spirit. I do not have to tell you that. But do not underrate your own contribution or your own service. You cannot measure the help that you render to others. You are touching souls, and this is among the most important work that can be done in your world.

The purpose of earthly incarnation is for the soul to find itself, for the divine spark to be ignited, to kindle it until it becomes a lambent flame. Alas, it does not always happen. Too many individuals live in the darkness of superstition and ignorance, and in a morass of doubts and fears and perplexities all the time. So if you can help one soul to find itself, you have justified your existence. Only one! That is enough. And you have done that for many.

How privileged we are to be in any degree the ambassadors of the divine. This is something the churches cannot be. They mouth ancient formulas which in their hearts they do not themselves believe any more. They repeat the stereotyped phrases and the worn-out ritual and ceremony that have long lost their meaning.

These churches, cathedrals and temples are sterile, barren and dead because the power of the spirit cannot function within them. It is the spirit which giveth life, and they deny the spirit, the Holy Ghost, time and time again. And so this divine power has to use those who wear no strange vestments, who stand in no pulpit, but who merely offer ourselves as channels for divine power to stream through us so that we can serve, and show that no one is neglected or overlooked in the divine plan.

When life was drear and dark, and you did not know

where to turn, when it seemed as if a blank wall of despair had come to stay, the way was shown. I need not say more than that. Love, affection, friendship, sympathy, compassion, pity, tolerance, these are the undying qualities. Love cannot die. Death has no power over life or love, and the other qualities I mention are in truth aspects of love. I am not speaking in riddles.

[*Silver Birch mentioned the spirit presence of Fred Jones, a great healer, and his guide, with whom Brother John once worked.*]

What a band is here to greet you! They helped to show you the way, they are still showing you the way. The healer is a great soul. The time came when his spirit was too big for his physical body, but he made his mark. He did his work to blaze the trail, and his pioneering efforts were not in vain.

Whereas in his earthly day there were but a handful to heal the sick, now their number is legion, and very necessary they are, too, in your ill world where there is sickness of body, mind and soul everywhere. Alas, the disease of materialism is very contagious, it is an infection which spreads and spreads. But just as light will drive out darkness, so healing will drive out disease by showing the individual how to live aright.

It is not doses of medicine, drugs and poisons that will promote health. It is not pouring filth into human bodies that will make them well; this is a form of medical lunacy. When you live aright, when your thinking is right, when the spirit, mind and body are harmonious, you will be healthy. The stresses and strains of your earthly life, its tensions created by selfishness, wrong thinking, greedthese are the poisons that choke the whole physical existence.

If I can urge you to go on, then it will have been worth your while coming. It is not easy, I know, but he who desires the prizes of the spirit cannot have the easiest of paths to follow. The Great Spirit is perfect, the natural laws are perfect, they cannot and will not fail. But within the framework there is an element of free will in which man has the chance to make his contribution. He cannot destroy the whole world, he can create much havoc in it, but there are limits to what he can do.

The divine plan cannot go wrong. If it did, or could, then the Great Spirit would cease to be great. Perfection cannot err. If it could then it would not be perfection. The divine ordinances of natural laws have always been in existence, they have never failed. Has the earth ceased to rotate on its axis? Have the tides. ever failed to flow? Has not night always followed day? Does not the fruit grow according to the seed that is planted?

No, life must pursue its divinely appointed path and plan, but man in his foolishness, ignorance and selfishness can sow weeds. He can choke parts of the garden. He must learn to live aright, that is man's contribution. He has within him the tremendous divine potential, but he has to learn to exercise it.

Brother John commented, after the circle, on how impressed he was with its simplicity and humility: "The simplicity with which the two worlds had become as one. The simplicity with which a great soul had taken over the body and mind of another, to expound simple but profound truths.

"And humility? There are many passages in Silver Birch's words which, to me, express this great quality. But even more salutary were three separate occasions during his conversation with me, when I spontaneously thanked him. Each time the guide, quietly and so gently, uttered those words with which he ended, 'Do not thank me, I never accept thanks.' Humility? I think so."

*   *   *

The manipulation of all this material, the placing of the right people in the right place at the right time, was quite a feat which required intricate, complicated systems of co-operation. Now, not my teaching, it is the teaching of the Great Spirit, reaches many. With others we are able to pour some light and power into your troubled world. When you come to me after all these years and tell me that something that was written in a book or a journal was of help, I feel all our labours have not been in vain.

SILVER BIRCH

Chapter Three

THE ALL-PERVADING POWER OF THE SPIRIT

If the power of the spirit could fail, the earth would cease to spin on its axis and the seasons no longer follow one another in orderly sequence. If the power of the spirit could fail, the sun would cease to be a fiery orb and the moon fail to reflect its illumination. If the power of the spirit could fail, no seed would flower, no fruit would grow.

SILVER BIRCH

The spirit which breathed life into us has given us a common link, because throughout the whole world all the children of the Great Spirit are fundamentally united. The spirit that enables them to live on earth and beyond is the same spirit that makes them a vast family with a common, divine parent.

It is this sublime truth we seek to express because it is greater than all physical differences, obstacles and barriers. It transcends all colour, language and nationality. It reveals that behind the surface of physical being, there is a common spiritual attribute that binds all people together with an unbreakable brotherhood and sisterhood.

This vital truth is necessary all over the world. When it is appreciated, it will help to end all war, it will destroy selfishness, greed and vested interest that are far too dominant in many lands. It will substitute the only true superiority, the advance of the spirit over the lower, debased material standards that are far too prevalent.

As this understanding spreads, so the infinite power of the spirit, with all its wealth, splendour, grandeur, love, guidance and healing will manifest in fuller measure and drive out the darkness of ignorance, prejudice and superstition that have reigned for too long and brought chaos and disaster in their train.

You are the Great Spirit in miniature. That power can grow, expand, unfold, enlarge, flourish, bloom, as you allow it to do so. You determine its growth, none else can do it for you; that is the purpose of earthly life. Realise that you are the Great Spirit and you realise that the kingdom of heaven is within you. It cannot fail.

You cannot want, you cannot go hungry or thirsty once you have adjusted yourself to the laws of eternal supply. You will not receive more than is necessary, but you will receive according to your growth, no more, no less, no higher, no lower. It cannot be any other way.

Spirit is not subjected to the limitations of matter. Spirit, which provides the dynamic of all life, the mainspring of all existence, will provide you with all that you require in your earthly life. The purpose of your being here is a very simple one. It is to fortify, to equip, to unfold that spiritual nature which is yours, so that you are prepared for the next stage beyond death. Thus, every experience, good or bad, sunshine and shadow, strength and weakness, love and hate, health and sickness, adds its quota to your spiritual growth.

There are millions of ways of expressing truth, because truth is of the Great Spirit and it can only be expressed according to the evolution of the individual through whom it has to be expressed. It is through simplicity that you learn truth. Using long words and finding new names does not make for truth. Often, they serve as masks for ignorance. The truth that we teach is the truth of the Great Spirit that knows no bounds and no limitations. It is for all, not for one. It seeks to embrace the whole of humanity within its loving embrace.

Reality is not to be found in matter, neither is it to be discovered within your bodily frame. The seed of existence is not to be located within any bodily organ. You are spiritual beings now. You do not attain spiritual natures by coming to our world.

From the moment of conception you are spiritual beings. There is nothing that you can do to cut yourselves off from that reality which enables you to live. The whole of your world exists because of spirit. Without spirit there is no life, for life is spirit and spirit is life.

Hold on to essentials. Do not allow yourself to be diverted. Hold fast to that which you know to be true and when all seems to be full of riddles, relax, retire within where the peace and power of the Great Spirit dwell. And within, in the silence and hush of the spirit, you will find all that is necessary. Make sure that that which is being woven into the fabric of your being is according to the divine pattern.

Let us remember why we were created by the Great Spirit. Let us strive to do nothing which will bring a blemish to that divine association, so that always we qualify for the benediction that comes to all who are linked in unity of purpose with the Great Spirit of all life.

*   *   *

It is the spirit which is the breath of all life, the spirit that binds us to one another and to Thee so that for all eternity we are linked with Thee in unbroken fashion. Nothing on earth or in the spheres beyond can sever the divine tie that makes us all members of one vast spiritual family.

SILVER BIRCH

Chapter Four

THE INESCAPABLE NATURAL LAW

If you can find a flaw in the natural law I will give up the whole of my mission. Show me where the natural law may fail to operate. No, it cannot do so. Effect always follows cause as an immutable sequence. You reap what you sow; you cannot have it any other way.

SILVER BIRCH

That which you call Spiritualism is part of the natural law. The Great Spirit has ordered the universe to be ruled and to be expressed through unchanging laws. These laws control every facet of universal activity. Nowhere in the whole universe, whether it be in those regions known to you or in that much larger portion which is beyond human reach, is there absence of natural law.

The divine will is imposed through divine ordinance. Most laws are subject to change and alteration, most laws are imperfect and do not take cognisance of every circumstance. But the laws of the Great Spirit have provided for every contingency that will ever arise. There is no happening left to chance or accident. All is regulated, all is controlled, all comes within the divine dispensation.

You have a physical body which is a machine. You are a spirit expressing yourself through the physical body. When you worry you close the sluice gates and the body loses the channels of its vitality. You cut yourself off from the source of supply. Until you learn that lesson, the body acts according to the natural law of action and reaction.

Worry inhibits your aura, which is your spiritual atmosphere, and disturbs the psychic vibrations. Until you remove the blocks the power cannot flow through. To attain selfmastery means a long and arduous discipline, a rigorous training, a constant refusal to allow your fear to dominate you.

The Great Spirit, with infinite love and wisdom, devised the law. The law is perfect, the law must operate. If you put the same energy you waste in worry into constructive thought, you would have no health troubles. The divine plan is perfect and you are part of it. You have to fulfil yourself. Opportunities of self-fulfilment are daily provided for you.

I cannot change the natural law. I cannot intervene in the unalterable sequence of cause and effect. I can only warn you when I see danger signs that the physical body is weak and therefore must be cherished. It is a machine and must therefore have attention. If neglected it must stop, so that with rest and recuperation it can resume its efficiency. You cannot cheat the natural law.

You express yourself through your body. You reach the limit when you step over the boundary, that dividing line when energy is so dissipated that the battery has to be recharged. This is your responsibility, because it is your body.

Much as I love you I cannot assume responsibility for your actions, words, thoughts. You are responsible for everything you think, say and do. As your body is the means by which you express yourself on earth, you must give it the attention that is essential for it to perform its labours. It is a wondrous, most complex, remarkable organism, far more intricate than anyone can construct on earth. It is a marvel of apparatus, but must have attention.

If you live in harmony with the natural laws you do not have illness, disease, or ailments. These are due to disharmony. Break the law and pay the price. Live within the law and reap the benefit.

Motive is of paramount consideration, but breaking the law must produce the penalty. It is for the individual, according to his evolution, to decide whether or not he will punish his body in order to satisfy his mind. Earthly life has its place in the divine plan. You should not quit the earth before the spirit is ready for the next stage.

Let us pose a hypothetical case of a noble person who is seriously concerned about the welfare of humanity and can make a contribution. Is he justified in damaging his physical body to make a supreme effort to do good in his own field? Only he can decide. It is unfortunate that often these decisions are actuated not by a single consideration. Sometimes there is an element of vanity, the feeling that the individual is indispensable in his field.

There are many sets of laws operating, some controlling the physical, some the mental, some the spiritual, some occasionally all interlocking.

It is sad that people do not appreciate the truths of the spirit until they have been reduced almost to the last stage of despair, when all seems hopeless. This is because far too many base their existence on a complete negation of reality. They think nothing else matters but the world of matter.

Somewhere the soul has to come into its own, to find itself, to become aware of itself, so that innate divinity can begin to be expressed. All this is part of the divine law of compensation. The greater the suffering, the greater the knowledge that comes as a result.

The Great Spirit is the greatest accountant in the universe. The books of life are always balanced, the adjustments are always made. So regulated is the divine scheme that spiritually you receive just what you merit, no more, no less. This is decided by the stage you have reached by your own efforts. In the things of the spirit there is always perfect adjustment, with no cheating or pretence.

The natural law works perfectly, guided by infinite love and wisdom. Each receives what he or she has earned. I did not make the natural laws, I only know how they work. This is cause and effect. No one can intervene between cause and effect. There are no accidents, no chances, there is only natural law in operation.

There is never any abrogation of natural law, neither suspension, nor interference. The natural law, is constant, it never varies, it cannot be changed. Live in harmony with the natural law and you reap the results. You cannot opt out of the natural law. It is supreme. The Great Spirit is the law in its sublimity, the epitome of law, not to be moved, not to be pleaded with.

We are grateful for all that has been vouchsafed to us, for the wisdom that has enabled us to have a clearer understanding of the universe in which we live, for the supreme power that directs it through natural laws and for the relationship between that power, ourselves and one another.

*   *   *

We have learned more about the working of universal laws and realise how they make provision for all that is essential to our wellbeing, that these laws, conceived by wisdom and directed by love, contain us all, make provision for our every need and are so comprehensive that none can be outside their orbit.

SILVER BIRCH

Chapter Five

LESSONS OF BEREAVEMENT

You should not grieve when death comes, unless you are grieving for yourself because you will miss a familiar face or figure. The spiritual verities should be the foundation of your existence. They should shine through your lives as radiant indexes to everything you do. You who call yourselves Spiritualists should not think that Spiritualism – the name given to certain aspects of spiritual truth – is something which applies only when bereavement is felt, and does not come into play on any other occasion.

SILVER BIRCH

Here, Silver Birch addresses in turn, a widower, parents of "dead" sons – one by natural causes, the other a suicide – and the widow of a famous journalist, Laurence Easterbrook, who was accompanied by her son.

'It has been a hard road, but you could not have done any more. You tried everything you knew. Who would want to try to perpetuate the earthly existence of one they love when the body can no longer hold the spirit? There must be separation at one time or another in earthly life. It is better for the stronger to remain and the weak to pass on.

You can count your blessings, for you were able to face your crisis with knowledge and not with ignorance. How much more difficult would your life have been if you had not this revelation of what the power of the spirit can do? You had added to you some extra years of happiness. For that be grateful, but you could no longer delay the spirit which had to quit a mortal frame which could no longer contain it.

She had mixed feelings. Sometimes she wanted to go, sometimes she wanted to stay, but the latter was only because of you and not for herself. She will have no more pain. She will never have to face old age, infirmity, weakness and all the defects which inevitably come to so many people when they are long past the prime. As the body gets weaker, the spirit becomes stronger.

When you are happy, she is happy. When you are depressed, she is depressed. It is a physical loneliness, but not a spiritual one. She is never really far from your side. She still regards it as her home and you as her husband.

You have faith, not credulous faith, but real faith founded on what has been revealed to you. Knowledge came when you were ready to receive it, to prepare you for what was inevitable. Let that knowledge be your base. Life has still much to offer you even in your world. You have not come to the end of the road. You have your own service to render, your own gifts to fulfil, a purpose to accomplish.

The Great Spirit is perfect justice, providing through natural laws retribution and compensation. The account is always perfectly balanced. You will not be forgotten, overlooked or neglected. There is a love that will guide, sustain and cherish you. Let that be your sheet anchor. It will enable you to remain firm and steadfast all the time.'

* * *

'Your boy is proud of you both because of the way you strive to serve by helping those who come into your orbit. What is important is the seed that drops into receptive soil. The one you received has grown into a beauteous flower. Your boy is delighted to see how naturally you accept spirit truths which have made so great an impact in your lives.

You had to find a great truth through a great sorrow. This was the touchstone, the means to enable you to find yourself when you were lost and it seemed there was nobody and nothing that could offer any help.

It is a fundamental spiritual truth that the soul begins to come into its own only when the individual has touched the lowest possible depth and nothing material can offer even a gleam of hope. When realisation dawns that there is nothing in the world of matter to which you can cling, it is then that the soul has its rebirth and begins to find expression.

Your earthly lives are not easy; they have never been easy. But there is a law which takes care of such matters, that those who serve will never want; their essential needs are always supplied. It is for them to exhibit, as best they can in their lives, the result of what they have experienced. They learn, by doing so, to strengthen the links that bind them to the Great Spirit. The more you strengthen the link, the deeper becomes the channel through which help and power can come to you.

The soul who knows has equanimity, calmness, resolution. It shows no fear, it refuses to allow anxiety to stay, it banishes the darkness of ignorance, superstition and worry. It knows that the power which gave it life, which rules the universe, which makes provision for all that breathes and moves, cannot fail.

What is important is that you should not fail the Great Spirit, so that your actions never betray the trust that is reposed in you because of what you have received, what you are receiving and for the wisdom that you have acquired.

Hold on to what you know. Be steadfast because of all that has been revealed to you. Face up to each problem, do the best you can with it, and forget it. Help will always come because those who love you, and are closer to you than they have ever been on earth, will see that you come through.'

*   *   *

'Every individual is personally responsible for what he does, for this is the natural law. Much as you love anybody else, you cannot assume the responsibility for his life. You cannot shoulder the results of his actions. This is cause and effect. If you make a mistake you must pay for it – I am talking about the spiritual law.

In your world you often see injustice, unfairness and inequality. It must be so because it is an imperfect world. But the law of the spirit is perfect. It is unfailing. Effect follows cause with mathematical, mechanical certainty, you cannot divorce effect from cause. Each effect is the natural result of a cause which in turn was a natural result of an effect.

This is an unending chain of events. If you could alter the sequence of cause and effect, or of sowing and reaping, and thus make it possible for the selfish to be as spiritually evolved as the unselfish, then you would be making a complete mockery of any divine justice. And so it always must be that you will reap what you sow.

You are responsible for what you do. You must take the consequences. You will make mistakes and you will pay the price for them. You should learn from them. You came into your world to make mistakes; if you were perfect you would not be where you are.

The mistakes and blunders arise from the nature of your imperfection. But when you fall down you can pick yourself up. Nothing is irretrievably lost. There is always a new day, a new dawn, with a new hope and a new possibility.

They preach in some religions that you can be absolved

from your responsibility, but it cannot be done. None but the sinner can expiate the sin. You cannot, by the recitation of any phrase, or any words which you describe as sacred, give absolution and eliminate the effect of a cause.

So, much as you love somebody else, you are not responsible for his actions. He must learn and, in learning, he will grow, evolve, develop and unfold. This is the law of life. Life is not static; it is a constant movement upwards, part of a progress that is eternal. You cannot put a period to perfection. You will strive through aeons and aeons of time to get closer and closer to it, but you will not achieve it. The achievement of perfection is an infinite process, it has been achieved only by the Great Spirit.

Do not worry. Worry produces a blockage in the channel through which help can come. I always say that you should cast out fear. Fear is bad for you; it creates a miasma; it engulfs you; it blankets you with gloom. These are conditions which it is very hard for the power of the spirit to penetrate.'

*   *   *

'I have Laurence here with me. He is very proud of you both. You have come through very well indeed. He wants you to know that just as he has revealed his ability to guard and protect you, so you should expect with confidence that he will finish the job. Have no fear for the morrow. Never allow fear to effect a lodgment within your being. There is nothing in your world to fear.

Laurence is always with you, because where love is he is. He is never absent from your heart or your hearth: He has left you physically, but he is with you spiritually. Those who are united spiritually will never be separated. How fortunate are you to have found such a depth of love and understanding and to have fulfilled the purpose of being complementary to one another, the two halves that make the whole, the real divinity so rarely found in your world, the marriage of two souls.

You should be proud of him, a great soul whose illumination was often visible even when he dwelt among you. He could touch chords and reach heights that are not given to many. He loves you both. His love encircles you like a band of steel. He will always be with you. He will guard, guide, sustain and cherish. If only what you have could be had by millions, what a different world yours would be!

So greet each morn with exultation, the herald of new spiritual adventures filled with infinite possibility and the chance to add to your lustre and to your attainment. Each morn gives the opportunity to quicken your spiritual growth, to develop the divinity within you and bring you closer to the source of all life.'

*   *   *

We are, all of us, seen and unseen, wherever we may dwell, included in a vast spiritual family, with the Great Spirit as our Father and each of us as His children. The tie of the divine spirit binds us all together and makes us one. Thus we feel we are richly blessed because so many of the barriers between the two states have been overcome. There is, as a result, a procession of enlightened beings who are able to make their beneficent impact on so many in the world of matter today.

SILVER BIRCH

Chapter Six

THE RESPONSIBILITY OF MEDIUMSHIP

Those who serve are always served. You will find that when the account is drawn up there is a credit balance in our favour. We will not fail the instruments who dedicate themselves. We always urge and encourage them to strive to the highest expression of the gifts which have been bestowed upon them.

SILVER BIRCH

Only a few months before the passing of Helen Hughes, one of Britain's greatest mediums and an old friend of Silver Birch, he spoke to one of her devoted companions when she visited the home circle.

'She is a great soul imprisoned in a poor, weak body which is gradually coming to the end of its road and very little can be done about it. When the body is beginning to serve its purpose, it imprisons the spirit more than it has done before. But she has fulfilled herself.

She has achieved what she came into your world to do. She has lifted up the hearts of many, many people, dried the tears of countless mourners and brought a smile of certainty where before there were only tears, grief and bewilderment. She can rejoice at the long road of service along which she has travelled, knowing that never, at any time, has she failed the power of the spirit.

She is a magnificent exemplar of what an instrument of the spirit should be. Never by word, deed, or even thought, has she in any way betrayed the divine trust which has been reposed in her. As a result, she has pointed the way for others to follow, set a standard which others can emulate, because she has shown what the power of the spirit can achieve when it has a dedicated, selfless servant with whom to co-operate.

She may not be rich in the goods of your world, but she is wealthy in the riches of the spirit and possesses bright jewels that will never lose their lustre which she has earned through her long, untiring service. You give her my love and the love of many here who are filled with admiration and gratitude for all that has been accomplished through her powers.

The power of the spirit, which she has revealed and demonstrated in such a superb fashion, will not leave her. It will stay as a constant, divine radiance. She will always be aware of what is in her midst and also round and about her. If we had a lot more like her our work would be easier, but, alas, as was said a long time ago, "Many are called but few are chosen."

Here, in contrast, is a splendid example of how Silver Birch can speak on the same subject without repeating himself. He is addressing two husband-and-wife medium teams, one British, the other American.

The gifts of the spirit are submerged for a long time and can be called into the beginning of their expression only when the soul is ready. This is fundamental in the pattern, that the soul first comes into its own only when the depths of sorrow, illness, crisis, have been plumbed and it seems as if that nowhere in the physical world is there to be found any help.

You cannot fund yourself when your existence is

untroubled, when the sky is sunny and calm and all seems smooth and placid. It is only when the storm rages, the thunder roars, the lightning flashes and the rain beats down that this wondrous spiritual awakening comes.

The path has not been easy, but this is good for you. Do not complain about difficulty; it is the spur of the spirit. Meet the challenge always with the knowledge that you have. The power of the spirit is greater than the power of matter. When confronted with problems, pause, let the spirit show the way and be determined that nothing will deflect you from the service that you were born to give.

You have helped many, you will continue to help many. You are on a path of service, accomplishing far more than is being done by dignitaries of the churches, however sincere they may be. You are bringing the truths of the spirit to those unaware of them.

You are helping them to fulfil the purpose of their being. You are helping them to find their spiritual feet. You are spreading knowledge. All this is divine labour. You should be proud that you are called into this service.

Life is full of problems. There are very few roses and mostly thorns. But the power that guides you is the power that created the universe, the power that is infinite. Pay no attention to the folly of those who should know better. Ignore the pinpricks and the jealousies. These are unimportant.

Try to feel sorry for those who do not measure up to what is expected of them. Anyway, that is their responsibility. Strive to discharge your duty as best you can. You are not called upon to do better than your best. Make yourselves as efficient instruments of the Great Spirit as you can. Strive so that even a greater measure of power flows through you and brings strength, guidance and love to those who need your service.

There is much work to be done in your world, especially today. The forces of evil are rampant, selfishness rules, vested interests defend their crumbling castles. If you help one soul to find itself, it is all worth while. Just go on.

Together, we can help those who need our help. Let us give it willingly, not force it on those who are unready, but to all who come within our radius. Let us help them so that they too may obtain an understanding which will enable them to fulfil themselves. And so the power of the spirit will continue to spread.'

*   *   *

I find it a privilege that you should want to come and talk with me – because you both have very evolved beings who use you as their instruments and they have demonstrated their ability to guide you in the willing service on which you are engaged. You are living exemplars of the power of the spirit at work. You are treading a path which has been chosen and, as a result, you are able to help many who have come into your orbit.

There is nothing new I can say to you; I cannot add to the knowledge you have received. It has been dispensed to you by beings in my world who are very advanced and who are respected for their spiritual attainments. But perhaps if you hear it from lips other than your own, you might find it some source of satisfaction to you.

What I would like to say to you, as a friend, as a cooperator, is that even with your own gifts you cannot be aware of the tremendous power which is round and about you. It is not possible, because you are restricted by being encased in physical bodies, to have a full awareness of this power of the spirit, the power of life itself.

You have been called because you have been chosen to do a work which is very important. I do not say this to flatter you. I am not given to flattery. You are helping the spiritual evolution of the world in which you live. You are helping the Great Spirit in the infinite processes of creation.

You are demonstrating fundamental realities upon which the whole of life is based. You are presenting the only way by which man can save himself and his world. You can demonstrate spiritual reality, the only unchanging factor in all life.

In a world which constantly loses its direction, you are part of the vast army engaged in the task of combating the materialism, which is your world's malignant cancer that poisons and erodes all the time. It is the parasitical growth which has to be destroyed because it is making humanity sick in body, mind and spirit.

The religious bodies cannot do this because the power of the spirit is not vested in them. They may have temporal power, but they have no spiritual power. They have no authority of the spirit which resides in the gifts of the spirit bestowed by the Great Spirit.

You can show those who are heartbroken by bereavement that death is the great liberator, that it brings freedom to the soul and that reunion is a certainty. Where there is love you can bring this truth by demonstration – the churches cannot do that.

When all the doctors have pronounced their verdicts of hopelessness you can bring hope because you can, in many cases, restore health. If you cannot cure you can alleviate, achieve betterment, give strength and vitality. And if you cannot do that you can help the soul in its passing from the physical body which has served its purpose. And that also is important.

In a world which chases after illusion and shadow, you can show where truth is to be found. And you can prove what you say, which nobody else can do. This is a great task; it is a divine work; it is the labour of the spirit; it is a tremendous service.

You must become weary sometimes. It is not easy to be a servant of the spirit in a materialistic world. Sometimes those who should be your greatest allies, in their foolish, stubborn pride become your enemies. You must be sorry for them. If they who have seen the light prefer the darkness, it is their responsibility.

You are the ambassadors of the spirit; you are the divine emissaries; you represent a power greater than anything in your world. And because of that, greater is your responsibility.

All I say to you is, go on. It will not be easy. The soul that is evolving does not seek ease. It demands the challenge that will enable it to bring to the surface its latent strength and emerge stronger in spirit as a result. It will be worth while. There is much work to be done, so many souls to be helped, so many who have lost their way, and nobody else can help them but you.

You will make mistakes, plenty of them, that is why you came into your world. If you had nothing to learn you would not be where you are. Yours is the schoolhouse where children come to learn their lessons. Were you perfect you would not incarnate into matter.

You live in a vast continent where mammon is worshipped as a greater priority than God, so you have much work to do. Wherever you pitch your tent the power of the spirit will be there and the light of the spirit will radiate. You will help souls who are brought into your orbit.

"Silver Birch was, as I expected, profound in wisdom yet so great in humility," volunteered one of the visitors. "Everything he said we both appreciated, but with me there was an inner knowingness of his reality that meant

so much. I saw him overshadow the medium, who seemed to disappear completely as the guide talked. In this work one can become weary at times. He provided the means to restore one's faith in one's purpose."

To the daughter of a famous medium and healer, anxious to begin her own Spiritualist ministry, Silver Birch said 'You must forgive me for leaving you to the last, but there is a precedent that says the last shall be first. I did this, not in seeming discourtesy, but I thought it would be easier for you to get used to the way in which I work and communicate.

In any case, I observe no feeling of strangeness, because you are fortunate enough to have been cradled in these matters. What seems strange and difficult to others has been natural to you. Not that it has been easy for you. The soul that is strong and independent does not seek ease and you had to make your own way. You have had to display a necessary independence so as to follow your own path and the dictates of your own reason.

You have been richly blessed. You have been the recipient of so much wisdom from a very great soul whom I know very well. This has helped you even more than you realise. Yet, despite all that, you chafe and are eager to do your own service in your own way. But the time has not yet come. The door has not yet opened for you, but it will.

I will let you into a secret, which others here know already. If you knock on a door and it does not open, do not push. If you push the door gently and it opens, that is for you. You cannot go through a closed door. Too many people in your world waste time and effort banging at closed doors.

You have seen how the power of the spirit works. When it has prepared what is necessary for you, there is nothing you need do except gently open the door. Meanwhile, serve wherever you can. There are always those to whom a service can be rendered. It need not be blatant. It can be the right word, the right touch, the healing thought, the healing action.

The power of the spirit, as a result, effects lodgment where before it was inaccessible. And so you become the human catalyst. As a result, the power of the spirit has made a little wider circumference because of your act. So much is in store for you that you can regard each day as a prelude to wondrous spiritual adventures. In the days that are to come your heart will sing and rejoice at the opportunities that have been presented to you.'

*   *   *

I think it appropriate to include in this chapter on mediumship Silver Birch's words to Ralph Rossiter, secretary of the Spiritualist Association of Great Britain, who has, despite many health setbacks, worked diligently to promote spirit truths.

'Always it is a source of gratification when people like you and your wife ask to come and talk with me. I feel you have so much knowledge and experience that there is very little I can offer you. Sometimes, however, the words that come through the lips of another instrument are confirmatory and enable you, in a different setting, to feel that you are more aware of the power that is always round and about you.

Those who labour unceasingly, by day and night, for the spread of these truths are sometimes so close to them that they cannot see the wood for the trees. It is good to pause for a while and take mental hock of what is happening. You cannot measure adequately what is being achieved because, unfortunately, you have no means of registering spiritual results.

You see many people come and go, some comforted, some healed, some cheered, some enlightened, some disappointed and some not touched because they are not ready. The ceaseless round of activity can sometimes tend to make you overlook the central, fundamental fact, which is that you are touching souls. You are enabling the divine spark within to be kindled and in many cases for the first time to come into its own.

The sad tragedy of your world is the millions completely ignorant of any spiritual truths. Even many, who regard themselves as religious and attend places of worship, have no contact with spiritual reality. So they are dead spiritually to all the richness and beauty, to the exultation that life can offer to those who live on more than one plane of being.

They are unaware of the earthly purpose, they have no knowledge of what it is they have to achieve before they leave it. Their values are wrong, as are their priorities, their perspective is out of focus, their standards are false. Their lives are sterile and barren, they do not fulfil themselves and they have lost their way. They live in a constant maze and cannot find the path out of it.

You provide a spiritual lighthouse, with its beams constantly revolving, penetrating the darkness, offering sanctuary where truth can be obtained by those who are ready to receive it. We always say that at the end of your earthly term, if you have helped one soul to find itself, then your existence has been worth while.

You can regard yourself as richly blessed in the knowledge that not one, but many thousands, have been able to discover life's secrets, to enjoy living to the full and be equipped, without fear, to continue beyond physical death.

I wish you could realise the greatness of the service rendered by you, your colleagues and those much maligned instruments of the spirit who are engaged in this difficult task of helping man to find himself. Despite all the difficulties, problems and hardships and the necessity to find the money, you have won through and will continue to do so.

If only you, and all who serve as a band, could be aware of the tremendous power of the spirit that accompanies you and of the many advanced, liberated beings who co-operate in this labour that is among the greatest that can be done in your world. It is not easy, I know, but everything that is worth while is the hardest to achieve.

Alas, the churches of your world cannot perform this service. They cannot touch the soul, they cannot quicken the divinity within the children of the Great Spirit. Here and there, one inspired man of God can do this because he is naturally qualified by his psychic ability. The rest fall back on conventional utterances, repetition of creedal beliefs and resort to expediency. These have no connection with the inspiration and revelation that emanate from divine sources.

What is important is that man should become aware of his true self and of the access he can have to the source of all being. He should know that the Great Spirit is not inaccessible, remote, far off, unreachable, but is within himself and that he has a spiritual armoury, a strength, a reserve, a potency on which he can call in times of difficulty and crisis.

Moreover, in addition to this tremendous potential within himself, he can also reach out to the infinite power of the spirit without. He can climb a ladder, on which, rung after rung, there are beings waiting to help him as he is ready to reach them. And this is important.

It has not been, nor will it be, an easy life for you. I would not be speaking the truth if I said otherwise. But this is the service you came to render. This is the debt that you have to pay. The torch has been handed on to you. Keep it bright, so that it can burn even more strongly when the time comes for you to hand it to others.'

* * *

From a Silver Birch invocation:

It is this latent spirit within man that we seek to coax into higher expression and by so doing enjoy the boundless beauties, the riches, lustre, dignity, grandeur and nobility that are the expressions of a divine spirit.

With the realisation of these possessions, man can uplift himself, sever some of the shackles that bind him to earth and enjoy the rich heritage of his unexplored mind and spirit. By this means he opens himself to inspiration, wisdom, revelation and truth, which are already streaming in increasing measure as man fits himself to be the recipient of this bounty from a larger life.

These are accompanied by the full flowing, magnificent and sublime power of the spirit, life-giving in essence, dynamic and vital, bringing in its train health for the sick, strength for the weary, guidance for the perplexed and light to those who are still in the darkness.

Chapter Seven

HEALING, THE GREATEST GIFT OF ALL

Healing is a soul process, not a physical one. When a soul is ready the healing will take place. It must be so, it cannot be any other way. Healing is the power of life applied to its receptacle, the soul in the earthly body. It is the stimulus, the rejuvenation, the reinvigorating power applied to the centre of life in the physical body.

SILVER BIRCH

Ulyndu and Amenra are the pseudonyms adopted by two healers who put into practice the precept of selfsacrifice. Both renounced their commercial careers to devote their time to healing the sick. The world is now their parish; they have worked in Central and South Africa and India. With complete dedication, they never charge for their healing, demonstrating in their daily lives "the unfailing source of God's supply."

Living from day to day on their travels, sometimes their money has completely run out and they have had to tighten their belts. But they say each day their needs were supplied with no prompting. Often the channels were "as unexpected as they were extraordinary." On a visit to this country from South Africa, they fulfilled a long-cherished dream, to meet Silver Birch, whose teaching they had followed for many years.

'Nothing affords us greater pleasure than to be of any help to those who are instruments of the spirit. If those whose lives are untiringly concerned with serving others feel that any words from me can help them, then I am privileged to be the mouthpiece of those who sent me.

We are all engaged in the same mission, charged with a duty of trying to help a sick world to heal itself, to prevent it from performing acts of reckless folly, to abandon practices of selfishness and greed that cause misery to millions and to allow the spirit to shine with lustre and beauty as is the intention of the supreme power.

I do not have to tell you that the road is not easy. I do not have to say that it is not strewn with roses. Suffering is an inevitable part of the progress and attunement of the soul. It is only in suffering that the soul can come into its own. The man who lives only on the surface of life does not give his soul a chance to find itself. The soul finds itself only when man has exhausted all earthly channels and seemingly believes there is nowhere else to turn.

When the extremity of matter is reached the spirit comes into its own and the tiny seed of divinity begins to grow and blossom and gradually to burgeon in all its beauty. Suffering is the other side of the coin. You cannot have light without cold, sunshine without storm. You know this.

You are richly blessed. You have never been overlooked, or forgotten, or neglected, or left entirely to your own devices from the time you set your hands to the plough of service and decided to follow wherever it went. It is a tremendous spiritual adventure that enables you to bring the power, the light and the healing of the spirit to those who otherwise would know nothing of its beneficence.

You are greatly privileged to be the instruments of the mightiest power in the universe. There is no mightier power than the Great Spirit. All it demands of you is loyalty, cooperation, fidelity, trust and perfect confidence founded on a faith which exists because of knowledge.

Do I have to tell you that long before you incarnated into the world you volunteered for this service? Do I have to tell you that all this was but a prelude, a training ground, a school to learn the lessons to be equipped and fortified and prepared to fulfil the purpose of existence?

Do not falter; do not allow at any time the slightest suggestion of fear to find a lodgment within your being. The power that has brought you where you are will not fail you. It cannot fail. If it could, the universe would cease to exist, for its motive power, its dynamic, its very sustenance would be withdrawn.

You are equipped with the greatest armoury of all, the power of the spirit. Let it be your strength, your haven, your refuge, your sanctuary and your ever-abiding inspiration. It will not lead you astray, it will seek only to inspire you to give the utmost service to those who cross your path.

You know that your material needs will be provided. You will not go hungry, you will not go thirsty, you will find the raiment that you need as clothing and protection. It will not be lavish, but the desire for luxury is not the hallmark of an evolved soul.

The physical body has primary needs which must be satisfied. The Great Spirit is aware of all that is required by bodies created to be the means through which this divine spirit would be expressed. Just go forward. Live for today and know that as the past proves the guidance of the spirit, so unerringly will the future enable you to give the service which you asked to perform.

Go on with your work. Raise up the sick so that they realise what has quickened them and made them well is the power of the spirit and nothing else. Then, if the healing touches their soul, you have gained a spiritual victory.

If the spirit is right and the mind is right, the body will be right. That must be so. The body is the servant, the spirit is the master. The body is the subject, the spirit is the king. Foolish people allow the body to be master and king. Their spirit never comes into its own to enjoy the domination which is its natural right.

Go forward. If anything that I can say encourages you, then I shall have considered it a great privilege to be the instrument for doing so. You are richly blessed to have the guidance of a being who has an exalted stature in our world. He is charged with great power and wisdom, and his understanding is profound. Try to earn the right to achieve the closest possible co-operation.

If you can carry your load with a faith born of knowledge, the load becomes lighter and it disappears. The trials and troubles that beset your path are challenges that you must face and conquer. You will come through and all will be well.

Do not allow any material circumstance, however seemingly large, to overwhelm you. There is nothing in the whole world of matter that is stronger than the power of spirit which gave it birth. You will come through. Your hearts will sing, you will see the pieces fall into their appointed place. Time is eternal. Your responsibility is to live for the now, for the moment.'

*   *   *

When true healing has been accomplished there can be no relapse. The law is unalterable, the law is perfect. I would not for one moment seek to avoid the exercise of compassion, mercy, kindness and tolerance which are all aspects of the spirit. But the law is neutral, automatic, inflexible, divinely ordained.

SILVER BIRCH

Rose Baston, faithful housekeeper and friend of Hannen Swaffer for over thirty years, is another who discovered her healing gift. She now has a sanctuary in Swaffer's old home at Clapham, South-West London, where they moved when he had to vacate his famous Trafalgar Square flat. Silver Birch dedicated it a few years ago. Here is his encouraging message on her healing work, when she later paid a visit to the home circle

"Ever since you invited me to dedicate your healing sanctuary it has established a closer link between us. It exists for the supreme purpose of helping the unfortunates and the sufferers. I do not have to tell you that your life is guided.

This is the purpose for which you were born. You had to wait a long time to be disciplined through difficulty and trouble, through treading the thorny path. You had to be tested and tried to qualify for the task for which you incarnated.

Now, as you look back, you can see how everything that has happened is part of the mosaic. There is a pattern, at first not to be discerned, but now revealing that all fits into its appointed place. How happy should be your heart that you are fulfilling yourself, acting as an instrument of the spirit, bringing relief, betterment and alleviation, not only of the body, but of the mind and spirit, a task which is more important.

Let the plan unfold as it has been doing. It is not easy. I do not think you would have liked it if it had been easy. Better to be tested and to win than not to be tested and so be unaware of latent strength and inner power. So many want a gift they have not got and take for granted what they have. But you were not aware of the healing power for a long time. When you were first told about this gift you were surprised.

It is not the ability to diagnose conditions that is important. Diagnosis, too often, is merely a physical assessment, whereas the root cause is not to be found in the body but in the mind and spirit. Don't be in a hurry, be patient. You cannot force spirit power. It can flow only as the channel is ready to receive it. It has to adapt itself to what is at its disposal. It is a very very subtle process; any attempt to force it does not help.

If ever you become dismayed, and it is very human to be cast down occasionally, just pause. Reflect on what has been achieved in seemingly miraculous fashion and know, because of what you have seen, the rest will follow. All that is asked is that you should discharge your responsibility with faithfulness and confidence in the power that has brought you to where you are.

Just do the best you can; strive for the utmost that lies within your power. There is nothing for you to fear. There are difficulties, but these will be surmounted. Each morrow that dawns is an opportunity for another spiritual adventure.

This is very important. Nothing will be allowed to interfere with that work. I know it is not easy, but the path of the faithful servant cannot be easy. You find yourself, despite your name, not on a bed of roses.

The soul comes into its own when it is confronted with a challenge. Then the dormant, latent strength and power can rise to the surface and be expressed. You have always been faithful to the light which was revealed to you. Never by a single action have you betrayed the trust reposed in you. We are all very proud of you."

Prizes of the spirit must be earned, they cannot be gained in an earthly lottery. The riches of the spirit come as you deserve them. As you unfold so automatically you are equipped to receive a little more than you had before.
SILVER BIRCH

Gordon Turner is well known not only as a healer but also for the great impetus his services gave to the National Federation of Spiritual Healers. He and his helper, Jo Prince, were particularly moved when they first met Silver Birch.

"Nothing gives me greater pleasure in all the years I have laboured in your world than to welcome here those who are servants of the spirit. I know the pattern which their lives on earth must follow. I know the heartaches, hardships, pains and the inner emotions which cannot be shared with the outside world. I know the price that must be paid, sometimes amounting to mental and spiritual crucifixion.

But this is the hard road that leads to spiritual attainment and to spiritual mastery where prizes have to be earned, where there are no short cuts, where every step that is really an advance has to be secure so that no retreat is possible. If it is an easy life that you want, then you cannot give service. It is only through toil, hardship, discipline and restraint that the soul comes fully into its own, to express itself as it is intended, to manifest those gifts with which it is equipped so that others who are drawn to you can be helped by those faculties with which the Great Spirit has endowed you.

But there is a corollary. It is not all sombre, dark and unrelieved gloom. There must inevitably be light and shade, cold and warmth, storm and sunshine, otherwise no advance is possible. The corollary is that as the soul comes into its own, latent gifts of the spirit begin to burgeon and their inner beauty is more and more outwardly expressed, so attunement with the divine is more closely established.

There is a reward which is the natural sequence of the law of cause and effect. It is the inner realisation that however stony the road, or prickly the thorns, or seemingly difficult the obstacles, the pilgrim is following his appointed path and gradually coming into his own.

You cannot measure what is being achieved. There are no instruments, no apparatus, no appliances in your world which can measure soul-growth and spiritual attainment.

You are bringing light to souls in darkness. You are giving food and drink to those who are hungry and thirsty. You are bringing the divine power, the life force itself, to bodies, minds and spirits that are presented with an opportunity to find true health. This is a wondrous service-and a great responsibility. It is not lightly that divine gifts are bestowed on human instruments. The measure of their responsibility is greater because they are the custodians of a divine power.

It is, alas, true that you are dealing with human beings. Sometimes those who should be your closest allies seem to become your most hostile foes. You become the victims of friction and misunderstanding even in the ranks of those who should be united by the same aims and endeavours. But it is not possible for all to see with the one single eye, even if they are engaged in the same pursuits.

It matters not what others say, think, or do. It matters only what you say, think, or do. The Great Spirit will not hold you responsible for the actions, words or thoughts of others. Your responsibility is to live in the light of what has been revealed to you. The greater the light the greater the responsibility. There are no escape clauses in this divine agreement.

The sick man is at a spiritual crisis when he comes to you. It is then he has to make the supreme decision. It is the turning point. Now he has a chance to begin to live as was intended. The sickness is a means of bringing him to spiritual understanding. If you heal the body and his spirit does not begin to express itself, then you have not succeeded, though it is not your fault. But if you can touch the soul, if you can allow the spirit to come into its own; then you are doing something no doctor, no clergyman, no scientist, no philosopher can possibly do.

You are enabling the seed of divinity to begin to express itself. As it does so, its association with the power that gave it birth begins to manifest and that soul begins to fulfil itself. Do not be disheartened if you cannot help all who come to you. The fact that they have come is their opportunity. You can only strive to serve."

If they think it is a good thing, a healer and his patient can tune in at the same time for absent treatments. But as the healer unfolds, and his development reaches a higher stage of attainment, it is not necessary. He has made his link. He can tune in and withdraw at any moment and allow the power to flow through him. I am not opposing the idea, but it is creating a limitation to say the power of the spirit will flow only at ten o'clock.

SILVER BIRCH

It is fitting to include in this chapter on healing, Silver Birch's comments on psychic surgery, as performed by healers in Brazil and the Philippines. From Mexico came a series of questions on the subject from its most prominent Spiritualist, Kenneth Bannister. After a successful commercial career, he devotes his time to healing and spreading psychic knowledge. Silver Birch readily became a one-man brains trust.

The success of an instantaneous healing depends on the patient's spiritual development, karma and other attributes. What happens in that respect in the case of a surgical "operation" as performed by spiritual healers in Brazil and in the Philippines?

All this is regulated by cause and effect which is the natural law in operation. Whenever the soul of the individual is ready, then that person is influenced so that he or she is brought into the region where the healer is to operate. If the soul is ready, then the operation is a success. But, whatever occurs, even if a growth has been removed and the body is now free, it does not automatically follow that the patient will spiritually come into his own. It only means that he has spiritually arrived at the stage where he is ready, and this is his great chance for the spark now ignited to be fanned into a flame.

So there are two factors in operation. The patient is spiritually ready, and that means he has been brought to the healer who can achieve the result. The patient now has the opportunity of spiritually coming into his own and living in the light of a spiritual awareness. If this does not happen then there has been a physical success but a spiritual failure.

Is that kind of spiritual surgical healing a good way to heal?

By their fruits ye shall know them. The wind is tempered to the shorn lamb. All the outbreaks of spirit power are conditioned to the place and the time when they occur. The whole of the operation of mediumship and the outpouring of the power of the spirit are part of a planned, concerted effort.

It is done primarily to meet the physical, mental and spiritual needs of the people to whom this applies. It is a question of temperament, education, environment, understanding, so that always the phenomena must take the form that will be most appropriate to those for whom they are intended.

Why are these spirit operations done in Brazil and the Philippines and not in Britain?

The spiritual climate is different; the mental environment is different. The needs are for more spectacularly striking results where minds are not yet conditioned to the more subtle influences of the spirit. It is somewhat similar to the conditions prevalent in your world just over one hundred years ago when it was necessary to demonstrate that kind of physical mediumship which would make the spiritual understandable in earthly terms.

It is not necessary to do this now in Britain. But it still obtains in those countries where the standards of education, culture and appreciation are vastly different from those prevailing in this land. It must be suited to the people who dwell there.

But there are a great number of people in this country who would very much like to see this type of operation and are unable to do so. Is climate an important factor?

It is partly climatic because the atmosphere is more conducive. But it is also a spiritual conditioning because it is not primarily suited for the people dwelling in your land. It is not a question of what people want to see but what is spiritually best for them. Too many prefer to have the highest spiritual elements reduced to the lowest physical level. This is not the way for advancement or progress.

The purer the instrument the more healing power can flow through him or her. Does that apply also in psychic surgery?

The question is not correctly stated. It is not true that the purer the instrument the more power can flow through him. Power can flow through an instrument that is not so pure. The quality of the power is affected by the purity of the instrument. Spirit power is infinite, like the Creator, the Great Spirit. Because it is infinite it has an infinite number of gradations, variations, combinations.

The individual tunes in to that stage for which he is spiritually ready. He cannot get any higher spiritually because he could not receive it and naturally he would not want to go lower. No, it is the quality of the power that is affected by the development, the attainment, the stage that the instrument has reached, not the quantity.

Would it be a good thing for all healers to be able to perform psychic surgery, even if it were possible?

No, there is not one road for all the instruments of the spirit. It is not uniformity that is desired but versatility and variety. Spirit is infinite and therefore has an infinite number of possible manifestations. It is all conditioned by the receptivity of the instrument. For that reason it is affected by the medium's temperament, upbringing, education, heredity, environment and even past incarnations.

All these affect and qualify the kind, amount and type of spirit power that can function through any instrument. It is not for all to follow the same path. You will find the answer in the Bible where it says, "Now there are diversities of gifts, but the same spirit."

What would healers need that they have not got now to be able to treat patients by psychic surgery?

You must not think in terms only of achieving demonstrable physical results with healing. Healing is primarily a spiritual happening. The object of healing is to touch the soul of the patient. If the patient's soul is ripe, the mind will be right and the body will be right. True healing leads to a correct alignment of spirit, mind and body so that they function in harmony. That is what health means, wholeness, harmony.

To remove a growth is not the objective, it is to touch the soul. You can have cancer of the spirit in that sense. Selfishness and all the wrong growths persist within, and until these are eradicated there can be no true spiritual progress. It is the spirit that must be paramount in all life. Until the spirit rules there will never be harmony, health, happiness or the fulness of living.

SILVER BIRCH

Chapter Eight

RELIGION – AS SEEN BY SILVER BIRCH

The very last place to find the power of the spirit is in the churches where it should have primary position. Man, no matter how high his ecclesiastical attainment, has turned his back on the source and foundation of his own religion and for some inexplicable reason prefers the bare, withered bones to the living truths of the spirit.

SILVER BIRCH

'It is sad that in the tune of your world's great need the custodians of religion are unable to speak with the authority of the spirit because they are completely insensible to its ability to manifest in their churches. Not only are they completely unfamiliar with the truths of the spirit, but their foolish beliefs have become so encrusted in their beings that they form an impenetrable wall which prevents the light of the truth, the wisdom and power of the spirit from effecting any lodgment within them.

How can the spirit find its way through all the hidebound ritual, dogma and doctrine which are so sterile? These churches are empty of the power of the spirit. And so you have the whited sepulchres again, the dried bones, the magnificent buildings, beautiful architecturally, but dead, cold, sterile, barren, because there is no illumination of the spirit within them. What is worse, they resist any attempt on the part of the spirit to make itself felt within their repositories, not of religion but a collection of dry theological doctrines.

I hope that does not sound too stringent, but it is the saddest of all that the ones who should be. the spiritual leaders are very much in the rearguard so far as these great truths are concerned. They are good men, who try to live blameless lives, but they are completely impervious to the very power of the spirit upon which all religion is based. Without the spirit there can be no religion. The spirit giveth life; where it is absent there is no life.

If the churches had fulfilled their purpose, if they had not departed into theological, creedal, ritualistic and ceremonial bypaths, it would not have been necessary for beings like us to return and restore those links which are essential if your world is to maintain its proper place in the divine scheme.

These men of God, as they are called, know the least about the Deity, the way in which the Deity works, or the natural laws which control the vast cosmos. And these are the foolish men who resist and oppose every attempt of the spirit to make its mark and work its beneficent will in the world of matter.

Why is it that these people will accept stories describing how the power of the spirit manifested centuries ago, but will not believe that the same power can manifest today? What they teach has nothing to do with the Nazarene. You are privileged, as are others, to do some of the greater things that the Nazarene said would be done, but this is regarded as heretical. If they knew how the Nazarene wept at the way the churches which are named after him continue to betray him.

The power of the spirit operates as part of a plan. For ages, it tried to be expressed through the religions of the day. Here and there a receptive instrument was found. The result was what the ignorant regarded as miracles, but which were vital demonstrations of spiritual laws at work. These were the same phenomena that you have witnessed in the presence of powerful mediums today, the same healing, due to the same spirit of which you are the instruments. It is the same spirit because it all emanates from an unchanging Great Spirit. It is as simple as that.

After each outburst of the power of the holy spirit, the men of the churches, the creed-makers, the theologians, the scholars, with their sophistries, got together. They replaced inspiration, which is divine, with formulas emanating in the minds of men, which, however learned they may have been, were bound to fail. The spirit gives life. All theology, by its very nature, is sterile.

After countless efforts had been made, the advanced beings in our world decided that the power of the spirit should flow outside the established religions because it could not make itself felt within them. There were raised up ordinary men and women, like yourselves, to become the vessels of this divine power, each in his or her own way demonstrating the same gifts of the spirit as the Nazarene did, producing similar phenomena.

No matter what the people who rule through churches, or chapels, the temples or synagogues may have to say, the power of the spirit is here to stay. None can banish it and none can thwart it. It will continue in ever-increasing power to encourage more and more throughout the world. That is what must be. Nothing will stop it.

I am all in favour of spreading knowledge of spiritual truths and realities, but I am not so concerned with institutions or with buildings. I am concerned with people, the children of the Great Spirit. As I see it, the divine plan is to help these children to come into their own, to understand their spiritual heritage so that they may fulfil their divine destiny. Our task is to direct individuals, to guide in the best possible way, with all the means at our command, so that they are brought to the stage where they are spiritually ready. At that moment the seed will begin to grow.

There are those who are concerned with influencing the men of the churches as individuals. It is right that any means should be essayed to help them to understand themselves, the power that brought them into being, the meaning of their existence and what it is they have to achieve before they quit the earthly scene.

Empires have risen and fallen. Dictators have come and gone. Churches have flourished and crumbled into the dust. The Great Spirit will go on, and the power of the Great Spirit will continue to manifest. There is no room for pessimism

If established churches do not see the light, then they will be obscured and enveloped by the darkness. It is good to try to spread knowledge. But I stress that the paramount task, as it has been shown to me, and I speak only for that which has been revealed to me, is to raise up individuals with the gifts of the spirit through whom this power can be made manifest.

How privileged we are to be in any degree the ambassadors of the divine. This is something the churches cannot be. They mouth ancient formulas which in their hearts they do not themselves believe any more. They repeat the stereotyped phrases and the worn-out ritual and ceremony that have long lost their meaning.

These churches, cathedrals and temples are sterile, barren and dead because the power of the spirit cannot function within them. It is the spirit which giveth life, and they deny the spirit, the Holy Ghost, time and time again. And so this divine power has to use us who wear no strange vestments, who stand in no pulpit, but who merely offer ourselves as channels for divine power to stream through us so that we can serve, and show that no one is neglected or overlooked in the divine plan.

True prayer is something that comes involuntarily from the heart. It is not an organised, automatic means of addressing the Great Spirit. There is no virtue in those who call themselves Spiritualists unless they are living in their lives the implications of the truth they have received. We do not worship labels. It is not what a man designates himself that matters; it is what he does.

SILVER BIRCH

Chapter Nine

IF SILVER BIRCH APPEARED ON TELEVISION

If you prefer blindness, keep your eyes closed. If you prefer deafness, keep your ears closed. But if you are wise, you will open the windows of your souls, so that you can become aware of that mighty, vast power of the spirit which will strengthen and encourage you and make you know how life can be lived and enjoyed to the full.

SILVER BIRCH

A sked what he would say if invited to speak about Spiritualism on television Silver Birch replied:

"I would begin by explaining that I am one of those whom your world of matter regards as dead, but that the beliefs of your world are founded on fallacy. Life cannot die. Life continues because it is part of the great, eternal, creative life-force.

I would ask viewers to put on one side all the misconceptions of their inherited prejudices and approach the subject of Survival with simplicity of heart and mind, seeking only to know the truth. I would appeal to them to be tolerant and sympathetic, not to worry about what others have taught, but to seek for themselves. I would cite as witnesses the many all over the world who know there is a life that continues beyond the tomb because they have spoken with the so-called dead.

I would say that I was one of those who, having completed my allotted earthly span and passed, many years ago, beyond the veil of mortal life, had decided to return to illumine your world and teach it the spirit truths which have been buried for too long.

I would outline some of those simple truths in simple language and ask whether my viewers thought they offended their reason or insulted their intelligence in any way. I would tell them that I have no vested interest, no money to earn, no job to defend. I have nothing to gain. I come back, after many years in the spirit world, to tell what I know. It is for them to listen.

I would say that you are deathless, that the ones for whom you mourn stand silently by your side-silent because you cannot hear them. You are the dead, the dead who are unconscious of life as it really exists. You have closed your eyes to all the beauties of the Great Spirit's universe. All around you the atmosphere teems with multitudinous life. Your own beloved ones are there and behind them serried ranks of the immortals, men and women from ages past, who, having served your world of matter, are still anxious to offer comradeship, guidance, fellowship and the wisdom of their extended experience.

The ties that bind you to the Great Spirit can be strengthened by your understanding. If churches stand in the way of your receiving that knowledge, discard the churches. If men are an obstacle, discard the men. If books stand in the way, discard them.

Retire into the silence of your own being; forget the world of matter with all its harsh discord. Tune into the subtle, delicate vibrations of the teeming spirit life around you. You can then transcend the limitations of the fleshly body.

Awaken to knowledge; awaken to understanding. You need not be a prisoner; you can leave the jail of ignorance and live in the light of spiritual freedom. Four walls cannot contain infinity. No book, however inspired, can contain all the truths about the infinite Great Spirit. No man, no matter what his degrees, can come between you and the Great Spirit.

You can obtain all that you require for your sustenance from the infinite storehouse. If you allow that divinity within you to rise to the surface and learn the laws responsible for the power and inspiration flowing from the higher spheres, you would begin to live as the Great Spirit intended you should.

Go into the world, try to heal the lame, help the afflicted, be a strength to those who have lost their way and give kindness and sympathy to all who need it. Then you are serving and service is the only religion. I know of no other.

Religion is the living of a life, not the acceptance of sectarian beliefs. The laws that control life are universal; where there is universal understanding, religion will be of mutual service. Whether it is called Spiritualism or not is unimportant. What is important is the spread of truth which destroys ignorance; the erasion of superstition when wisdom flourishes.

Beware of labels. More importance can be attached to the label than the truths it seeks to represent, when men begin to worship the label and not the truth. Truth is all-important, the label does not matter. More important than comforting the bereaved, than drying the tears of mourners, is the application of spiritual truth to all daily life.

Ours is a practical religion, a religion for every day, for twenty-four hours of every day, for sixty minutes of every hour and for sixty seconds of every minute. That is the standard we set, the ideal to be achieved, the true task of all those who have found knowledge.

Spiritualism must be judged by its results. If none is richer because of your presence in the world of matter, then you have failed. If Spiritualists do not make their weight felt in all the pressing reforms that are so vitally necessary, then they are false to themselves and to the inspiration which seeks to use them for that purpose.

The power of the spirit which is poured through human instruments has a mighty destiny to achieve. This destiny is regeneration. It is a slow process, but it is the only way humanity can advance. It is a constant enlarging of the sphere of illumination, a constant struggle against the forces of retreating darkness. You do not require another Nazarene. If the Nazarene himself were to return, he would be one of the most unpopular men in your world, especially among those who say they follow him and acknowledge his leadership.

You cannot alter an inflexible law. There is no cheap reprieve, there are no easy pardons. Divine justice rules the whole universe. A spiritual dwarf cannot pretend to be a spiritual giant. There is no death-bed repentance.

SILVER BIRCH

Chapter Ten

YOUTH QUESTIONS SILVER BIRCH

Rejoice that while you are comparatively physically young, you have this wonderful opportunity. How sad it is that too many still live in shadows, chasing will-o'-the-wisps, embracing illusion, failing to find reality. You are the repository of infinite possibilities. How much you can take will depend on you. That is the measure of free will. How far you can travel, only you can decide.

SILVER BIRCH

I reported the moving confrontation between four earnest young Spiritualists and Silver Birch in Psychic News. The guide invited representatives of the newly-formed Psychic Youth Group to the Hannen Swaffer home circle, asking them to come armed with their most difficult questions. The group had a special session to prepare their queries.

Four original founders, two boys and two girls, all in their twenties, attended the sitting, where their spokesman relayed the questions to Silver Birch. The contrast between their youthful enthusiasm for making a quick spiritual impact on this sluggish material plane and the tolerant guide, who over the years has been asked similar questions many times, was really a "happening."

One told me afterwards that he was deeply impressed by the economy of words and the flow of beautiful phraseology.

"It was as if every word was carefully chosen, yet the spontaneity of his replies was terrific," he added. In modern idiom, he said it was like feeding questions to a "spiritual computer" bound to produce the right replies. "Appreciating the true simplicity of Silver Birch's words, one can absorb them like a sponge and it helps in answering future tricky questions on the subject," he said. Here, in question and answer form, is this Youth Group séance.

Many young people, like ourselves, seek truth. We want a better world in which to bring up our children. Why must man kill and maim his brother? Why must he hate those of a different race or creed? Why is there so little love in the world? We want peace on earth, but when and how will it come? How can we succeed where the older and so-called wiser have failed? We are young, strong and willing and wish to serve in the war against ignorance and stupidity, greed and hate. What then is your advice to us?

That seems quite a question. Ignorance and stupidity, the words you use, have been in your world for a very long time. There is no magical formula that will abolish them overnight. Nature works by evolution, not by revolution. All growth proceeds slowly and inexorably. Any attempt to force physical growth beyond its ordained limits inevitably results in disaster. Similarly any attempt to accelerate spiritual growth must fail.

I say this in no spirit of pessimism. I know that all those who have been permitted to catch a glimpse of spiritual, divine reality must be optimistic. They realise that man, however foolish or reckless he may be, has imposed on him restrictions. He is subject to natural laws over which he has no control.

There is no instantaneous panacea that we have to offer. All, we can say is that as knowledge spreads and ignorance, as a result, recedes, so the divisions between man and man become fewer, the wars abate, the greed lessens and the areas of light increase. It is not within our power to transform the earthly scene. All that we can do is to inculcate into those who are ready to receive knowledge the truths that will teach them how to order their lives aright.

Man has, again within prescribed limits, a freedom of choice. He can share with the infinite power in the processes of creation and help in the forward march of evolution. He can hinder, he can delay, he can deter. This is his contribution.

The Great Spirit, with infinite wisdom, did not create puppets, marionettes or automatons. Man was endowed with latent wisdom and with all the divine attributes that the Great Spirit, or God as you call it, possesses. So man must make his choice. He must learn that war solves no problems, but only creates fresh ones, that greed and selfishness contain within themselves the seeds of their own disasters.

Many years ago the Nazarene said that he who takes to the sword shall perish by the sword. Man must learn these lessons for himself. All that you can individually do is to spread knowledge wherever you can. If you succeed in bringing light and truth to one in addition to yourself, then your earthly life will not have been in vain. This is the only answer I can give.

We must be honest and say that the Spiritualist movement and mediumship in general are at a very low level...

Stop there. We are not concerned with what you call the Spiritualist movement. We are concerned with individuals who are prepared to develop the gifts of the spirit, whether within or without organisations is not very important. Organisations should perform or fulfil certain purposes. It is for the organisers to concern themselves with that problem. Our responsibility is always to help any individual who desires to serve wherever he can.

Names do not bother me. Spiritualist, Theosophist, Rosicrucian, these are only labels. What matters is that each should seek the truth according to his capacity. Mediumship is important because it means that here is a person on whom has been conferred a gift which can be used to give one of the greatest services in your world. It is a tremendous responsibility and imposes, or should do, a sacred trust on its owner.

To what would you attribute the sudden increase in drug-taking and addiction, especially among young people? Can we offer any tangible aid to them?

Yes, you can offer healing, the power of the spirit. This is always directed to the spirit or soul of an unfortunate being who has resorted to what could be dangerous drugs and who can be helped. You must try to realise that the power of the spirit is also the power of the Great Spirit, which is the life force.

It is the vitality, the dynamic, the mainspring of all existence. There is no life without spirit. Everybody who moves, breathes or thinks, does so because of the spirit. In healing, the life force is applied to the weakened vitality of the individual whose body, mind and spirit are in disarray through the intake of certain drugs. These have caused this disharmony, and thus there is a blockage, an impediment where natural channels should be flowing freely and harmoniously with one another.

If you have the gift of healing, you are a channel for this divine power which can stimulate, in the way that you charge a depleted battery, and enable the life force to flow again, rid itself of the impediments and blockages which have brought ill-health to the individual.

This is a much greater contribution than giving the individual another drug to get rid of the previous one. As to why so many resort to drugs, this is very simple. They are in despair, they are frustrated, they are pessimistic, they see no hope for themselves, they are out of touch with reality, they have lost their spiritual way and they can find in materialism no support for them. They look to the drug to give them a lift, but it is not the way. As I said before, nature works by evolution, not by revolution.

How can we young people best channel our efforts towards healing the rift between coloured and white people?

Only by example. If you show by your own lives that to you there are no yellow, red or black souls, that bodily skin has no relationship to soul qualities, then you will attract towards you those who are subjected to these bars, bans and barriers. The Great Spirit, with infinite wisdom, devised it that all His children should possess many coloured hues, so that together the perfect family make the rainbow. A white skin is no evidence of supremacy of spirit, neither is a coloured skin evidence of an inferior spirit. The real test is when you exhibit qualities of divinity, that is when the spirit is supreme.

What are the spiritual aspects of heart-transplant surgery?

Motive is always the important consideration. Undoubtedly in some cases the motive is to sustain earthly life. It can be that experimentation encourages an enthusiasm for more experimentation which in the end is not concerned with the prolongation of earthly life. Also it must be said that subjecting helpless animals to cruelty in order to learn from them is not an act that can be considered to have any spiritual value. Not through cruelty will man find health. Not through exploitation will he learn the secrets of nature that have so far eluded him.

I am not in favour of the transfer of any bodily organ from one to another. Indeed, I am not in favour of the transfusion of blood. I do not think, from my point of view, and I speak only for myself, that the sustaining of the physical body must be the be-all of every endeavour. I maintain that man should be instructed how to live aright, spiritually, mentally and physically. If he thinks right, then he behaves right and his body will be right.

The solution is not the transfer of bodily parts. The solution is for every man to order himself to live as the Great Spirit intended. Man must have compassion for other men and for all the creatures with whom he shares this planet. They were not placed here by the Great Spirit to be used as experiments, to prolong the physical life of man.

Is it right to say at this stage that heart transplants must be doomed to failure?

It is conceivable that there may be some successful experiments. What I am concerned with is that the experiments are taking the wrong spiritual turning. This is not the direction in which those who should be dedicated to man's well-being should be working. They will not bring health. Health is harmony. These are merely attempts at a temporary patching up of bodies.

You must understand the simple essence. You are created body, mind and spirit. These are indivisible; they are not exchangeable parts. You are a whole individual. To achieve health you must have wholeness, harmony, rhythm, concert, between your tripartite being. This is the only way that you can get health, not through drugs, not through medicines. These are temporary reliefs. Your world is full of ignorance. Death is the dread monster to be evaded. Death is feared, but death is part of the natural law. Physical immortality is not the object of earthly existence. The earth is the training ground, the school to learn your lessons for the greater life that must inevitably be yours.

How would you describe God?
    It is impossible to give you a complete picture. God is infinite. All language, concepts and pictures must be finite. The lesser cannot include the greater. You can obtain some idea of what the Great Spirit is like by looking at the universe. See how it is regulated by natural law, where provision has been made for every facet of life, even though these manifestations are multitudinous in their variety. Whether it be minutely small or majestically mighty, all that lives, moves and breathes, all that exists, are controlled by natural law. Nothing is outside the orbit of natural law. The seasons follow one another, the earth rotates on its axis, the tides ebb and flow. Whatever seed you plant, what will grow is contained within it; it will be true to its nature.

    Law reigns supreme. Every new discovery, whatever it may be, wherever it may be, is controlled by the same natural law. Nothing is forgotten, nothing is overlooked, nothing is neglected. What is this power responsible for it? It is infinite. It is not a magnified man, the Jehovah of the Old Testament. It is not a deity who is full of vengeance and sends plagues because of displeasure. It is not a capricious, wrathful deity. History and evolution show that the world slowly moves forward, upward, revealing that the power behind it is beneficent. So gradually you get this picture of infinite love and wisdom that rule all, that govern all, that direct all and are within all. And that I call the Great Spirit.

Another question that crops up many times is the thought of returning to God. There is a certain fear that you lose your individuality in this return.

The ultimate is not the attainment of Nirvana. All spiritual progress is towards increasing individuality. You do not become less of an individual, you become more of an individual. You develop latent gifts, you acquire greater knowledge, your character becomes stronger, as more of the divine is exhibited through you. The Great Spirit is infinite and so there is an infinite development to be achieved. Perfection is never attained, there is a constant striving towards it. You do not ever lose yourself. What you succeed in doing is finding yourself.

Is it possible to describe this state we are supposed to reach?

No, because you get to conditions and spheres that are beyond language. They consist of states of consciousness and awareness. This is something that you will not understand until you attain it. You do not lose your individuality in a sea of greater consciousness, but that depth of the ocean becomes included in your individuality.

To what extent does destiny play its part in man's earth life? Could you describe destiny? Is predestination an outside force or your own choice? If you accept reincarnation, can you say why and what purpose it serves?

It could be both. An outside force helped you to make the choice. You can have free will and destiny at the same time. If you are content to accept that earthly life is the sum total of physical existence, then so be it. But it is conceivable that the spirit which inhabits your present earthly body has existed before, with not necessarily that facet of the spirit. It could be that you are a fragment of a very large diamond, with each facet incarnating at differing epochs to make their contribution to the whole.

You mention a facet of a large diamond, that I could be one of a group soul of people. It does not seem logical, if we have eternity, that it would be necessary for me to have experience for a number of other souls.

Action and reaction occur throughout the whole universe. Men in far-away places can produce a tremendous impact on your existence in the way of contributing to the sum total of knowledge everywhere. You cannot live in physical, mental and spiritual isolation. Call it a group, call it a diamond, you are trying to use words to express what is beyond words. Who are "you," and when did "you" begin? Did your individuality commence from the moment of conception? "Before Abraham was, I am," said the Nazarene. What did he mean? Only that as spirit he had always existed; so have you and so have I. It may be that fragments incarnate at differing times.

I have no quarrel with those who will not accept what I say. I always tell my friends to reject what their reason cannot accept. If we would win your affection, and perhaps your love, it must be because reason tells you we say what is true. If we cannot win your affection with reason, then we must be failing in our purpose. We must build on the knowledge that we have, making sure that its base is secure. From that, let us explore the higher paths as we ascend, slowly, gradually.

You have much to make you rejoice. Problems you will always meet, difficulties you will always encounter. You are not perfect beings living in a perfect world. You are imperfect and your world is imperfect. But you have free will and a wonderful opportunity of helping to rid the world of its imperfections and yourself of your imperfections. That is your task.

Whatever knowledge you have gained, the greater is the responsibility as to how you use it. A trust is reposed in you. You must not betray it. You must show by your own life that you are worthy, not only of the knowledge that you have received, but ready for the next knowledge to come to you as it will when you are ready to receive it.

Always there will be offered, as you are ready, a vast richness of the spirit which cannot tarnish, fade, or ever be lost once you have acquired it. These are the prizes for you to earn, the development of your own soul, the strengthening of your own character, so that you are worthy of the light in which you dwell.

SILVER BIRCH

Chapter Eleven

ASPECTS OF ANIMAL SURVIVAL

It is not part of the plan that needless cruelty, torture and brutality should be inflicted on animals by the humans who believe that they have a superior consciousness and are much greater beings. All life is one. The divine spirit animates all who share this planet and have responsibilities towards one another. You cannot divide life into watertight, rigid compartments. All aspects of life, man and animals, must move forward together. The animals cannot be left behind while man makes his evolutionary ascent.

SILVER BIRCH

A well-known Spiritualist couple, who devote their lives to animals, acknowledge that their acceptance of Survival helps them in dealing with their "lesser" brothers, who are more psychic than humans. Michaela and Armand Denis, famed for their "On Safari" television programmes, have attended the Hannen Swaffer home circle several times. Silver Birch, naturally, spoke to them on the subject closest to their hearts. Here are extracts from their sittings, combined with the guide's comments on animal survival and welfare at other séances.

'It is not possible for you, whose spiritual faculties are hindered by physical senses, to measure the results of your labours. You have pioneered in what was originally an arduous field and demonstrated that there can be a kinship between man and animals, and that mutual respect, toleration and compassion are part of the divine law of evolution.

Man's place in your world is not to uproot, ravage, destroy, kill or to maim. It is to live in harmony with the whole of creation so that the stronger helps the weak, the more knowledgeable helps the ignorant, and those who arc in the light should strive to decrease the area of darkness in which others dwell.

You have been able to show by your labours what is the rightful place that the animals should occupy in the great plan, and by doing so you have spread knowledge, which is one of the main essentials to be accomplished in your world. It is unfortunately true that too many of the problems, disasters and tragedies that occur in your world are due to stupidity and conceit.

Compassion must reign; toleration must be enthroned. Harmony, not destruction, is the ideal to be achieved. When man wages war on other creatures, be they human or animals, he retards his own evolution. Nature cannot be at peace when man is at war with them.

It is only through amity, concord and co-operation that peace will come throughout the world. Until this is achieved, the earth will continue in travail and disaster will follow disaster as man interferes instead of co-operates. As man uses the creative principles with which he is endowed, when he lives in harmony with the whole of nature, then peace will come to the earth and the beginnings of the heavenly kingdom will be founded in your world.

Cruelty begets cruelty, war begets war, but love begets love and compassion begets compassion. You get what you radiate. If you fill the world with hatred and destruction you reap destruction. Sow the wind and reap the whirlwind.

With love in your hearts to all, with malice towards none,

and that includes all creatures, you can help the processes of infinite creation. This is the great contribution that you can make in the vast evolutionary scheme of which your lives are part.

Never be discouraged in this field of labour. You will meet misunderstanding, stupidity, foolishness, ignorance and cruelty that is both wanton and innocent. Your weapons must always be the knowledge of the underlying spiritual realities, the purpose for which all live to fulfil themselves, so that they can share in the generous bounty which nature provides if man's greed did not dominate his thinking.

You have many gifts. You and your husband have still a great contribution to make in the cause of helping animals. You cannot ignore any integral part of the living creation, for all are bound inextricably in the one pattern and plan. You serve those for whom you are ultimately responsible because you share your evolution with them. You must march forward with them, to ensure that they too develop as they should and not merely be the creatures of suffering and exploitation.

The whole of creation is knit together and man's responsibility extends beyond his own kith and kin, for he has dominion over the beasts of the fields and the birds in the air. Thus he should prevent the cruelty directed towards helpless creatures who give him no offence.

It is not part of the divine plan that animals should be slaughtered so that their carcases may be used for the adornment of human bodies. All cruelty, especially needless cruelty, must be abhorred. Those who champion the rights of dumb creation must continue to fight, always appealing to the moral principle that is involved. He who is cruel to a bird or a beast will be cruel to a man or a woman.

Let those whose hearts are stirred and whose pity melts at the spectacle of cruelty, continue to labour valiantly, knowing that in the end triumph will be theirs. Much cruelty is done in ignorance, but when the eyes are opened and knowledge comes, cruelty will be abolished. Once you are receptive to truth you become receptive to other aspects of that truth. If your spirit is awakened and touched, you start on the road of enfranchisement.

In the long line of evolution, at some stage the Great Spirit breathed into the animal and it became a living soul, conscious, aware of its own existence. Then came the dawn of reason; intelligence bloomed; there was judgment, the ability to reflect, to decide, to weigh and to consider. But potentially all that existed-no matter how far back in the line of evolution you go. It required the breath of the Great Spirit to awaken it.

Just as the Great Spirit enabled a divine spark to become a flame, so you, by love, transfer that process to the animal who lives within the shelter of your affection. You are part of the Great Spirit, having the power within you to transfer the attribute of spirit to the next in line of evolution. By your association, by radiating love, you awaken that consciousness which in time, through the process of evolution, would reach its own apex.

At some stage the animal and the human evolution inevitably part company. It may take, as you measure time, hundreds of thousands of years, but their rate of spiritual evolution is unequal. The animal has to be left behind because it cannot keep pace with the growing soul that restlessly struggles towards the greater light.

Once you have passed from the veil of matter and accustomed yourself to conditions of the spiritual life, once you have realised that the ties which bind you to earth are severed, the desire to progress, the desire to unfold the surging divinity within becomes quickened. You seek to unfold all the 'qualities which, by their practice, will enable you to be of greater service wherever you are. The higher you climb in that realm of spiritual unfoldment, the more difficult is it for the animal to keep pace with you. And so the love which kindled for a while a flame that burned beyond death gradually becomes attenuated. The flame flickers and it merges in the end with the group soul of that species.

Although there is one general evolutionary scheme for all creation, it takes different paths according to its manifestation. There is a group-soul for those animals who have not attained that kind of individual consciousness which man has attained. Some animals have been enabled to attain their individual consciousness in a form similar to man through association with him helping to advance that individuality.

Where you have a group survival, it is not a static process, but a constantly evolving one. If man were aware of his responsibilities to all creation, as higher beings are aware of their responsibility to man, then the animal evolution would be accelerated and become more individuated. But until the link becomes closer, the paths are separate, though to some extent parallel. With the process of evolution, the group souls would become fewer and there would be more individual souls.

There is the kinship of the spirit that is the common nexus in all life. Where there is life, there is spirit. Man's ferocity is reflected in the retarding of animal evolution, just as man's brutality retards his own evolution. The processes are similar. All life is intended to be of mutual helpfulness, by co-operation, by service to one another.

Motive is the important consideration. If in order to end physical suffering, when any beloved animal is beyond all earthly aid, you put a period to its physical life, your motive is a good one; and thus the motive qualifies the passing and helps. But if, with complete and callous disregard for all the natural rights of animals, you kill them, then your motive is selfish. You do no good to yourselves or to them, and they have to be helped. They have compensation for what they missed on earth, just as children, who are either stillborn or have had very little earthly life, are provided with a compensation for what they should have enjoyed in your world.

You are dedicated to the service of helping those who are unable to help themselves, the animals whose love and fidelity, trust and devotion are unfortunately too often repaid by a remorseless cruelty and torture by those who do not realise what they are doing. This is a great stain and foul blot on what you euphemistically call civilisation. As savage as the Red Indians, as we were supposed to be, is the treatment accorded to the beings who, animated by the same spirit as you are and who share the same path and evolution as you do, are cruelly exploited and made to suffer.

It is no accident that you were called into this service because the hall-mark of spiritual attainment is compassion. Without compassion there is no spiritual progress. Compassion must be extended to all beings, to all animals, to all creatures, to every manifestation of the divine spirit that exists in your world. Those who have moved a little further on the road of progress know they have a duty to everybody and everything that is an integral part of the world in which you live.

No matter how strong the opposition, how seemingly great the obstacles or difficulties, no effort for good that is made can ever be lost. Ultimately the fight in which you are engaged must be won because in the end truth must triumph. It is not an easy path which you tread, but pioneers and dauntless souls must not expect a bed of roses, or imagine that they will become lotus eaters. The greater the soul the greater the tasks that it is called upon to perform.

I do not have to tell you that apart from the colleagues' who serve with you in your world, there is a battalion of comrades who co-operate with you in our world, beginning with the man they call Saint Francis, who is actively concerned in this work today. There is a long line of pioneers who bend their whole being to this crusade and who are still engaged in striving for success to lift this scourge from your world.

Sometimes those who should be your friends become your enemies. Sometimes, alas, those in this field forget its purpose and place self before service and think that the individual is more important than the cause. When that happens, shed a silent tear for them because they have lost their way.

All that you are asked to do is to be faithful to the light which has been shown to you. If you have the single-minded purpose of giving service, than which there is no higher religion, then automatically you call to your aid the tremendous power of the spirit which can remove obstacles and allow the beneficent will of the Great Spirit to be expressed in your world.

There are two paths of evolution. One is the physical, in which man, the species, has evolved from the animal ancestry. The other is animal evolution in its present physical form. The whole of life in all its aspects is intermingled and interdependent. There is a close relationship, a kinship, because all life is spirit. Being infinite, it has an infinite number of manifestations. No aspect of spirit can be cut off from another aspect.

Some animals have been able to attain individual consciousness in a form similar to man through association with him. It is not possible for the human to confer an individuality on the animal, but he can quicken what is latent, just as you have meditation and other practices which can release your own innate spiritual qualities. Only the Great Spirit can confer the eternal qualities that are within every sentient being.

The soul of an animal is exactly the same in essence as the soul of a human being. Both come from the same divine source. The difference is not of kind but of degree. There are separate, parallel laws of development for animals and humans. They branch off when they have accomplished the purposes of their incarnation and its immediate after-effect in our world.

Thus both have functions to fulfil. The human sheds more and more of personality, the bodily expression of an individual soul becomes less and less of a human as more of the spiritual nature is unfolded and the latent perfection finds greater expression. You become less of a personality and more of an individuality as you draw closer towards the perfection that only eternity can achieve. Similarly the animal continues its association with the human so long as there is a purpose to serve by it, so long as the love which brought them together exists.

All the species have their part to play in your world and in ours. Nothing exists by chance or accident. The perfect planning of the Great Spirit has ensured that every creature, every form of life, has its own contribution to make. There is no such thing as any species being placed in your world because it was not required and therefore has to be physically exterminated.

The infinite mind devised the whole creative scheme and ensured that each had its part to play in a comprehensive whole. That is why it is wrong for man to become the most destructive of all the creatures.

It is becoming more usual for wild animals and human beings to live together. It is the barriers of fear being broken by love. If man had not slaughtered and murdered and terrorised, there would be no fear on the part of the animal world. Where it is helped, not physically, but psychically, there are animals who will seek for an association with humans that will help one another on the evolutionary path.

But remember that evolution is not in a straight line. You have the ups and the downs; you have a spiral. Sometimes it seems as if you are rising to blessed heights and at other times you are falling to diabolical depths. But nevertheless the plan is unfolding and evolution is fulfilling its place.

As love comes into its own, all will dwell together. It is man the destroyer, man the killer, who poisons the world in which he lives and sows the disharmony and the chaos that breed troubles. These are all his making, not the Great Spirit's, not the animals', but due to the misuse of his free will and his imagined superiority.

It was never part of the plan that man should consume his brother or sister in whatever form life manifested itself I do not have to tell you that animals who are slaughtered do not willingly accede, especially as some have sensitiveness and awareness. This abnormal death, like all sudden shocks, involves a process of adjustment. If man were aware of his responsibilities to all creation, as higher beings are aware of their responsibility to man, the animal evolution would be accelerated and become more individuated.

SILVER BIRCH

Chapter Twelve

OUTSIDE THE CIRCLE

I regard it as a privilege that you should ask me to come and share what little knowledge I have with you. If, because of this extended experience, I can be of some help then I shall be richly rewarded for having been in your presence. You all have a knowledge of spiritual realities and so there is no need for me to impress upon you their vital importance, especially in the world today.

SILVER BIRCH

After many years' devoted restriction to his home circle, Silver Birch has recently accepted invitations from Spiritualist organisations, meeting them on their own ground for question-and-answer sessions. Here are reports of his sittings – they were all tape-recorded – with council members of the International Spiritualist Federation during a congress at Copenhagen, the National Federation of Spiritual Healers and the Spiritualist Association of Great Britain. I start with the session for the International Spiritualist Federation.

'From our point of view this is a very good opportunity to put yourselves in proper focus and perspective. All of you who are engaged in this great labour so often get caught up in the day-to-day details and problems that it is not surprising that occasionally you lose the pristine beauty of the grand vision that inspires the whole purpose of our coining together. It is very difficult for you, who are encased in matter and have your obligations to your physical body, to remember that always, primarily, you are spiritual beings. The divine power flows through your nature. Many of you have been endowed with divine gifts, the gifts of the spirit, that can be used in the service of those who are less fortunate than yourselves.

It is not an easy path that you tread because you are of the calibre that wants the chance to bring out the latent qualities within you. For the servants of the spirit there are no beds of roses. For those who wish to evolve and to advance, to attain and to attune themselves to the highest reaches of our life, there is no easy way, no short cut. It requires arduous discipline, constant meeting with crises and the determination to fulfil the task on which you are engaged and on which – and here I become controversial-you all decided to engage before you came into the world of matter. This is the path that you have chosen to tread.

The spiritual race cannot be easily won. Spiritual supremacy is a long and arduous process. The prizes once gained are eternal – they are never lost. The prizes of the spirit will never be stained, they will never rust, they will never be corrupted. They will be yours for all time. These are the eternal possessions which you, each one of you, must acquire for yourselves.

Much as we, who are associated with you, love you and would seek to guard you and guide you and show you the way in every predicament, it is your path. You must pursue it, emerging from each difficulty stronger in spirit as the result and more qualified to fulfil the tasks on which you are engaged. So, welcome the challenge of difficulty. Those who do not want difficulty are of no use in the service of the Great Spirit. When war is being waged, and we are engaged in the greatest war of all, the war against materialism, it must be certain that the generals and the officers will not run away in the heat of battle. They must be tried and tested, and tried and tested again, so that they will endure and continue to fulfil themselves in thus divine but self-appointed task.

The forces that are arrayed against us in your world and in mine are very powerful. But they are not so powerful that they can prevail against the will of the Great Spirit. I tell you with all the authority that I can command, and I have worked in your world for many, many years and have been privileged to see a little part of the divine plan, the power of the spirit is here to stay in your world. There is no power vested in matter, or in those with influence in the churches, in newspapers, with doctors, or in any combination of these forces, that will be able to vanquish the power of the spirit which is in your midst.

In each land, where there are instruments of the spirit, bridgeheads have been established and are being consolidated, so that everywhere the children of the Great Spirit can find out for themselves who they are, what they are, why they are in your world and what they must do to fulfil the purpose of their being.

You have come from many lands, separated by vast distances, seas and oceans, but the power that has brought you together is the same one that inspires us all to give service. For ourselves we want nothing, no glory. We only desire to serve, to teach the children of the Great Spirit how to live so that they may realise the fulness, the richness, the beauty, the exhilaration which comes when spirit, mind and body function in harmony. You have the priceless opportunity of service and there is no religion greater than giving service to others.

This is the love of the Great Spirit in action. It is this love, this wisdom, this power, that has brought us all together in this land at this time, so that we may help to fulfil the divine plan of which each of us is a part.

So do not be dismayed if sometimes it seems that the battle is a strong and long one and that you get weary. When that happens, withdraw. Pause, reflect, let yourself be recharged by the inner divine battery. Let new life and vigour and purpose fill your being. Then, strengthened, go out and continue to serve.

I am very grateful to you for giving me this opportunity to voice these ideas which are not mine, but are the words of those who have sent me, as they have sent others who co-operate with you, to enable you to realise how we are all united in the divine plan.'

We have a big problem inside our movement. We have not the necessary unity, which we should have, to be very powerful. It is my great concern to find a way to better this condition. Have you any comments on this?

You will not achieve this very easily. Unity cannot be ordered. It can be achieved only by gradual growth as understanding comes. One of the great difficulties is that the whole of mankind is at different levels of intellectual, moral and spiritual attainment. There is no one common standard. Even in your own movement you have many clashes based upon the simple fact that each is at a different stage of evolution. Spiritual realisation can come only with advancing spiritual attainment. What is so clearly patent, when you have established that unity with higher beings, is not something you can share with others who have not reached that stage. Therefore you must attempt to accomplish the greatest good with the means at your disposal.

This is not a problem unfamiliar to us, because we are confronted with it all the time. We have to work with earthly beings some of whom do not measure up to the standard that we would like. And so we have to do the best we can. You will find gradually the light does spread. The important factor is that you organise gatherings, like you have had here, where people of different ideas and languages, from differing lands with different traditions and environments can meet and learn from one another. They see, for example, what others have achieved, so that where they are backward they receive the stimulus to advance. Do not worry. Do the best you can. When you can do no more, relax and let us take over. You are only asked to do the best you can, no more.

Could you perhaps point out a better way?
There is no better way than the truth. The problem of reincarnation, for example, is one of the difficulties that you will not resolve. Here, again, it is not a question so much of trying to obtain conviction by what is called evidence – these are only words. Conviction comes only from within. When the soul is ready it knows – that is the only conviction that matters. Science is constantly changing and enlarging its boundaries. Knowledge is not fixed, but conviction is the inner realisation that you at last have come face to face with truth.

You will not get agreement, not for a long time, if ever at all in your world. To those who accept reincarnation, it is so simple and so easy. And to those who do not, it seems so difficult. You must be patient and wait. It will not destroy your organisation. It is good that they will argue and that they should disagree. Nature abhors a vacuum. Inertia is contrary to the law of nature. Action and reaction are both opposite and equal but part of the same power. You cannot stand still, you must argue and discuss. Out of the melting pot, out of the cauldron, when the seething and the bubbling subside, truth will gradually emerge.

Could you tell us anything about reincarnation?
I have the same difficulty as many of you experience.
While I accept it, my instrument does not. If I have not
succeeded in convincing him, I will not succeed in
convincing others.

You could tell us if it is the truth or not.
For those who know, it is a truth; for those who do not
know it is not a truth.

*What is your opinion about our connection with different
faiths? Should we tolerate those who try to infiltrate our
truths? Or should we go our path alone and estrange
ourselves from them, as some people want to do? In my
view knowledge of Spiritualism should be infiltrated into
the churches, tolerating their activity. Spiritualism should
help those with little faith to become more religious.*

These are words that you use, like Spiritualism, but we are
concerned not with words. Words are an attempt to clothe
ideas and realities. We are concerned that the power of the
spirit, of God – use your own words but I call it the Great
Spirit – shall make a lodgment in your world wherever it
can. That is the purpose behind everything that we do. Why
do we want the power of the spirit to effect a lodgment? So
that it can touch souls and bring them into life. It does not
matter where this is done, in a church, outside a church, or
in the home. It is the individual soul that should be touched,
wherever you can reach it.

Those who are ready to be awakened out of their
materialistic sleep will come into your orbit, or you can go
to them and try to plant the seed of the spirit. If you fail,
shed a silent tear-not for yourself, but for them. They have
had the opportunity and alas they have not taken it. But here
and there the seed will fall into ground that is receptive.

And it will begin to grow, to flower and to burgeon into beauty and grace because it is the seed of divinity. Then the soul is beginning to come into its own.

The whole purpose of earthly life is that man should live on all aspects of being, physically, mentally and spiritually, and until these three are functioning he is not fulfilling himself. If he is living only with his body and mind, he is chasing illusion and shadow and missing reality. But when the soul begins to come into its own, it opens the door to tremendous spiritual possibilities and adventures for him. That is why he incarnates into your world of matter so that the soul should come into its own.

So it is not important that it should happen in this or that place, but only that it should happen. This is the reason for suffering and pain in your world, so that the individual should reach that crisis when matter can offer him no more and he is ready to turn to the spirit. "The wind bloweth where it listeth," as it says in your Bible. Let the wind blow where it will. Where you meet with receptivity, help as much as you can.

Could you give some advice on what changes should be made in the presentation of mediumship and Spiritualism?

There are new aspects emerging all the time. The physical aspects of mediumship are gradually receding and the higher aspects of healing and teaching are gradually emerging because of a differing cycle of evolution in your world. Just go as you are inspired. There are no cut-and-dried formulas for spiritual attainment. You must allow yourself to be led by the same power which has brought you where you are now. It has not failed you. It has brought you here where you are in possession of priceless knowledge which is more important than all the material possessions of your world. Just go forward, do the best you can wherever you can, and you will be guided and sustained.

I am very interested in linking the world of spirit with our different language groups in South Africa. Do you have a system whereby, coming nearer to groups like this, you can pick up vibrations in colour, form or shape in which the different languages are expressed?

This is something you must do in your own land, where you have this problem. Language is only an artificial means of trying to express thoughts, ideas, imagination and other aspects of inner reality. You will never succeed in finding adequate words. You must do the best you can by trying to win the souls of these people. You must touch them, come with a message that awakens them, comforts them when they are grieved and heals them when they are sick. You will find that when they are ready, you can do things for them. When they are not ready, you can do nothing.

There is no easy road in these matters. It is largely trial and error. We are not perfect. We are constantly learning new techniques in communication, in the handling of spirit power, in the mixtures of various forces to be transmitted through different instruments as they evolve, grow and develop. It is not a fixed arrangement. The whole thing is fluidic, because spirit itself is infinite and thus capable of infinite manifestations. I haven't answered the question in the way you asked it, but have tried to answer it in the only way I can see it.

Are we making serious mistakes in our approach to the world in general? If we are, could you enlighten us on these mistakes?

If you never made mistakes, you would not be on earth. That is why you are there, to make mistakes and to learn from them. If you were perfect, there would be no need to incarnate. You are there so that you can learn, and that is part of the law of evolution. But evolution is not a finite process, it is an infinite one. The object of evolution is growth towards perfection. But perfection is infinite and cannot be achieved. It has been achieved only by the Great Spirit, who is infinite love and infinite wisdom.

The more perfect you become the more you will realise there is further perfection to be attained. It is not a static process. The law of evolution is working itself out through all its manifold stages and these are happening concurrently. Man's physical evolution, despite what scientists say, is not yet over. It has many forms yet to be expressed. Similarly the mental and spiritual evolutions have a long way to go, even on earth, before they attain the stage which they should reach as part of the threefold purpose of man's incarnation.

You must recognise that this is an endless process in your world and in the whole universe, in itself evidence of the infinite intelligence which has devised the whole scheme, with wondrous laws that never fail and which provide for every facet of being everywhere to be guided, sustained and regulated. All of us are within this scheme of infinite love, law and wisdom. So go on making mistakes, learning from them and getting better spiritually all the time.

Here is the session for the National Federation of Spiritual Healers:

"The object of healing is a very simple one. It is to touch the soul. If you physically heal the body and do not awaken the soul, the healing has failed. If you do not heal the physical body and you touch the soul, the healing has succeeded. As far as we are concerned, all gifts of the spirit, and the power of the spirit, should be exercised to create an awareness of the divinity that each child of the Great Spirit possesses, so that there comes the recognition of the purpose for the earthly incarnation.

This is the whole object behind every phase of what is called mediumship. So you must never be distressed if you find that a sufferer does not get physically better. But what you must be distressed about is, when you have given the healing, if it has not brought an awareness of spiritual reality to your patient. This is the supreme purpose behind all healing.

We have banded together in our world to ensure that the power of the spirit, which has bridgeheads in many countries, should be consolidated so that divine power is available to those who are ready to receive it. Always our directives are to the essential, to create the awareness within individuals of who they really are and what they must do to fulfil their purpose. To put it very simply, we want them to know their spiritual origin so that they can achieve their spiritual destiny.

The gift of healing is part of one of the faculties that lie within the spirit body. It is like clairvoyance, which is seeing with the spirit eye, and clairaudience, hearing with the spirit ear. To be a healer you have to be accessible to the power of the spirit.

Let us be clear about the terms we are using and try to define them. To me, the Great Spirit is the infinite intelligence, the supreme arbiter of all life, the acme of all love, wisdom, truth and understanding, but not a person. I have to use your words and say "He" and "Thou," but the Great Spirit is not a deified man. The Great Spirit is the life force, the dynamic, the vitality, the consciousness, the animation. The Great Spirit is the epitome of all those principles. The Great Spirit is infinite. The spirit power is infinite too. None can have a monopoly of the Great Spirit or the power of the Great Spirit. It will stream wherever it can find channels. You can no more have a monopoly of healing than can the churches or Christian Scientists.

All you can do, if you have the gift of receptivity, is to develop it, to achieve a greater attainment and attunement. The power is infinite. The amount that you can receive depends upon your stage of evolution and development. Your receptivity determines the limit of spirit power that flows through you. It is as simple as that. You increase your capacity to receive and greater spirit power will flow through you, and greater results will be obtained. The whole process is fluidic, it is not fixed; but we do not understand all the conditions required to achieve success. There is constant experiment in our world, the mixture of varying forces, the compounding so as to achieve the greatest possible results with the material at our disposal.

You cannot put a period to the amount of spirit power that can flow. The only obstacle is the stage of development that you have reached, and that determines what you can receive. Now this divine power, the power of God, the Great Spirit, life, whatever you like to call it, is able to flow through you, the human channel, because you have the power of receptivity. Then it has to go to the patient.

Perhaps I am being elementary if I say to you that the cause of all sickness, illness and disease is disharmony. Health is wholeness; health is when there is the right rhythm and balance between body, mind and spirit. If they are not in proper alignment, if the focus is wrong somewhere, there is an interference with the natural vitality and so you get illness. The spirit power cannot flow through and perform its task.

Man's diseases are psychosomatic, which means they begin in the mind and the spirit. I don't have to tell you, who have experience of this, that a patient who is always worrying will get ulcers and that cutting out the ulcers won't stop him from worrying. You have to teach him to teach himself how not to worry.

You will find that nearly all illnesses begin in the mind and the spirit, and even many physical so-called accidents can also have a mental and spiritual origin, a premise which will plunge us all into very deep waters indeed. What do you do? You, the healers, receive spirit power which flows to the spirit, the consciousness of the patient. You are the battery, the stimulator, you recharge the vitality that has been depleted. You clear the blockage; you get rid of the impediment; you restore the balance. The rhythm is now in concert and harmony again.

Then the healing succeeds because you touched the spiritand this is the vital point. It is not putting your hand on the body that does anything. That is only a means of contact, which may or may not be necessary depending on the stage of attunement that you have reached. But you have to touch the spirit, you have to quicken it, you have to awaken the slumbering, dormant spirit so that it begins to have the expression which was intended for it by the natural law. And if you do that, then all the natural, self-recuperating processes of the body get to work and health begins to result. You have performed your function because you have opened the channel for God, the Great Spirit, to flow through you and touch the God, the Great Spirit, within the sufferer and brought him or her to an awareness for the first time.

This is what is involved in spiritual healing. I say to you, and here I am very serious indeed, you have a great responsibility. You cannot have knowledge without the responsibility that knowledge brings. You cannot have a divine gift without the responsibility of seeing that you use it in the way that is intended. There is a difference between psychic faculties and spiritual gifts. You can be a psychic healer or you can be a spiritual healer. In the latter case you have to order your lives to achieve the highest ideal that is possible. You have the gift, but its unfoldment is your responsibility. The way you use it is your responsibility too because the possession of the gift makes you one of the ambassadors of the Great Spirit.

You are more a minister of the Great Spirit than any minister of any church or chapel. You are representing the Great Spirit because the divine power is flowing through you. And that is a great responsibility. You must not sully it; you must not tarnish it; you must not dishonour it; you must not corrupt it; you must not attempt to use it for the wrong motives. You must only have the desire to serve and to reach out to the highest that is possible for you."

Can you tell us the manner in which that power is created on your side of life, that is, the power that is characterised for particularised conditions with people who are ill?

This is very difficult because it is hard to find words to describe non-material forces. What you have to try to realise is that spirit power is the life force, the stuff of life itself. It is animation. It is infinite. It is malleable. It can take a myriad different shapes. It is capable of an infinite number of permutations and combinations.

We have people in our world of varying degrees of knowledge, experience and understanding. We have the equivalent of what you would call chemists and scientists, who are forever blending aspects of this life force, this power of the spirit, to characterise it, to use your word, which is a very good one. They are always experimenting so that it can be conditioned to the greatest possible extent through the instrument, who is the channel, and bearing in mind the nature of the complaint or ailment which is to receive the healing.

I do not think I can put it any other way. It is an individual process for every sufferer who comes to the healer. The aura of the patient helps a great deal, because this gives a perfect picture of the spiritual and mental conditions which are responsible for the ailment in the first place, and this determines the blending that has to be done.

Does it require a mental effort on the part of those in the spirit world who are able to do this?
Mental is not the right word, because it is very real; it is an actual blending. We use the spiritual equivalents of what you would call chemicals. The mind has to be used because in our world the mind is the reality for building everything

Bearing in mind the effort of absent healing, to what extent are we used, either our physical or spirit body, in contact healing for this spirit power?
But you are used in absent healing too.

Are our physical or spirit bodies used in absent healing, or are we simply used because of our attunement to make the link?
Your spirit body has to be used for the absent healing.

Can you explain the process?
You are like a television set. The spirit vibration comes to you and you transform it into the semi-physical healing ray to the patient. You are the transformer.

In absent healing as well?
Yes.

Then how does it get to the patient?
Because the patient has made a request to you. Thought has created the vibration to you. There is the link, and through you it goes back on the same wavelength.

How about if the patient doesn't know that absent healing has been asked on his behalf?
Somebody must know otherwise you would not be giving absent healing.

Well, you might know that the patient is not very well and you decide to give absent healing.
Then you have got the link there.

But you haven't got the thought coming in.
Yes you have, you have created it. You must remember that thought is real on our plane of being. If I look at you, I don't see a physical body. I might if I could open the medium's eyes. It is your thought that is real to us, your body that is shadowy. The moment you send out any thought, that is a reality, that creates a vibration, a wavelength, and this is used in all the absent healing.

I know that faith isn't necessary in the patient for him to receive healing. Am I right in thinking that if a patient's mind is filled with unkind thoughts towards others that can prevent the healing?
I don't object to faith, as long as it is founded on reason and is not blind faith. You who have this knowledge realise that what you have received is only an infinitesimal fraction of the totality of truth. It is not possible whilst you are encased in mortal bodies to receive all knowledge. You will not get it even when you come here. So you must-have faith founded on what has been revealed to you. Now

a reasoned faith, founded on knowledge, is admirable. I have no quarrel with that, because it creates the right atmosphere of optimism in which results can be obtained. The power of the spirit works best when you are bright and happy, cheerful and receptive, not when you are miserable, doubting, wavering and disturbing the atmosphere around you.

Where healers are unable to see the aura, in what way can they work to know they have got the right attunement?
It does not matter whether the healer can see the aura. It does not matter whether the healer is able to diagnose. The object of the healer is to heal. He should not concern himself with these other matters. He has to make himself accessible. He has to be as perfect an instrument as he possibly can. He has to outlaw from his nature all the weaknesses that prevent him from being the perfect instrument. And the more he does that, the greater will be the power that flows through him. It is the life you live that qualifies the attunement you can have.

Many healers are fortunate in being able to improve their gift by attending circles of instruction. What advice would you give to those who have no facilities for such development? Furthermore, do you consider that mediumship is essential to good healership?
To answer the second half, a clear emphatic "No." The gift of the spirit is the gift of the spirit. You are born with it and it is your responsibility to develop it, just as the child born with the gift of playing the piano has to develop it by practice and training. How to develop this gift? It is not the answer to sit in circles. That may help. It is developed by your motives. It is developed by the way you live your life. It is developed by the attempt to reach the highest standard

of purity and perfection that is possible. It is helped by increasing your desire to heal as much as you possibly can.

The only way to develop self is to forget self. The more you think of others, the better self you will become. There is no book that will tell you how to become a better healer. What you have to do is to desire to serve, and order your life in this fashion: "The Great Spirit has endowed me with a gift for healing. May I be worthy of it." If you live your life according to that principle, the gift will automatically increase in its strength and stature.

What makes one person a better healer than another?

The same thing that makes one person a better speaker than another, a better pianist than another, a better writer than another. The gift is nearer the surface.

If a man is a healer, must he depend on another healer, or can he do anything to help himself if he becomes ill?

You need not depend on another healer, but you have to learn how to attune yourself to the power so that it can produce the result on you direct. Just as you do not have to go to church to pray to the Great Spirit, so you do not have to go to a healer to get healing, if you can enable the power of the spirit to come direct to you. You must open your heart, your mind, your soul.

Doctors say that some of the major sicknesses are due to pressure and business worries. In such cases how much does disharmony contribute?

You are saying the same thing as I said in different words. You are calling it a business worry, but that is a disharmony. If your mind, body and spirit are in the right relationship, you do not have worries of business or anything else. The soul that worries is out of harmony already. Anyone who has knowledge of spiritual realities should not worry. Worry and fear are the negative forces. They do not belong to the enlightened soul. You call it a business worry, I call it disharmony. There is nothing to worry about once you know you are an eternal being and nothing in the physical world can touch your soul.

Why are some people not healed?
Because they have not spiritually earned the right to be healed.

Once a contact has been made for absent healing, is it necessary for it to be made again?
Not once the link is made. Every link with our world is a magnetic one. Once made it cannot be broken.

So it doesn't matter where you are, whether you are in a church or in a railway station.

The world of the spirit has no geographical location. It is round and about you all the time. You are no nearer the Great Spirit in a church, or in a pit, or in an aeroplane.

It has been said that nothing material on our plane manifests but what it is preceded by thought. In other words, we build a thought matrix. Does it help if a healer mentally visualises the perfect healing as he tries to approach his patient and builds the image of perfect health?
It helps tremendously because your thought is a reality. The more you think of perfect health, the closer you come towards attaining it. You should always strive your utmost for the ideal. You should always visualise the best. You should never abandon hope. Always radiate cheer and optimism. These are the conditions in which spirit power produces its best results.

You said just now that a person has not been healed because he has not spiritually earned the right to it. That seems to me rather an over-simplification, suggesting that if he is a bad person he would never be healed and a good one will always be healed.

It is not as simple as that. This is too facile because you have to remember you are not necessarily looking at the problem with the eyes of the spirit. To you, suffering is terrible. To us, it can be divine. To you, disaster is the end. To us, it is sometimes the beginning of a new life. You must not bandy these terms of good and bad as if they are fixed objectives based upon a material evaluation. Our standards of appraisal are not always the same as yours. I say that a person must have spiritually earned the right to be healed. I did not say that he was good or bad. Once the spirit has come into its own, it has earned the right to be healed. The healing will be effective.

Does this answer always apply to healing and non-recovery? Are there not sometimes conditions that do not heal for purely physical reasons? For instance, a nerve within the body is totally destroyed, perhaps affecting the vision. One would not expect that within the laws that govern us it can be made a completely new nerve again.

We are not talking about miracles.

Yes, but I thought you were generalising on the reason for nonrecovery.

I am saying that where the illness is capable of being healed, and the results are not obtained, that patient has not earned the spiritual right to be healed.

A baby has two deformed legs. One responds and the other does not: why is that?

Because the healing cannot produce results in both cases. The healing is never equal, it is always conditioned. It is characterised. It is very difficult because I want to keep this on the simplest possible plane. There are other qualifications, because there are laws within laws within laws that involve other and more profound issues.

Healing is not as simple as it appears. It is not a question of just healing a physical ailment. It is soul qualities that have to be measured. What is the effect on the soul? What is the purpose? Why does the patient go to the healer? Has that patient reached the stage of spiritual evolution when his spirit can be awakened?

These are matters you cannot measure with your material yardstick, but they are all involved in healing because you are handling the life force itself for the time being. You are partaking in the process of infinite creation. That is why I stress your great responsibility.

Can you tell us what causes someone to become or be an epileptic?

There is a disturbance in the brain which makes it impossible for it to register and to have the correct stimuli from the mind of the individual.

But can it be cured?

Of course, every disease can be cured. There is no such thing as an incurable disease. There are only people who could be incurable.

On three or four occasions when I have been asked to give absent healing I have been unfortunate to be, in my way of thinking, unsuccessful. Each one has passed over.

This may be the greatest success that you have achieved. If you have helped a soul in its passing, that is a successful healing. The object of healing is not to prolong physical life. It is to touch the spirit. That is what matters. Get your first things first. It is the spirit that matters. If the spirit is right, the body will be right.

I have noticed with surprise, that some healers take a few minutes in their work on patients. Others perhaps take as long as two hours, some, weeks and others go on month after month, year after year, and the person seems to get no better. Can you explain it, please?

By their fruits ye shall know them! It is the results that matter. The healer should so live his life that he attains the greatest pitch of attunement. Then the results will come. You put your own house in order first. We will do the rest. No call for help is ever refused. No power is ever withheld. We always strive to serve. We refuse none. We welcome all. The power of the spirit is there for all to receive its benificence. All we want are willing instruments to help its divine flow.

A person gets healing and improves, but later passes to your world. Why is this?

Why is passing to our world a tragedy? In our world, when people are born into yours, we cry. When they come to our world, we rejoice. Why is it a tragedy to leave your earth?

We have every sympathy for the mentally sick yet we feel so helpless.

You can help the mentally sick. If you allow yourself to be used, that is all that is asked of you. Let the power flow through you. Those you cannot help by contact, send them absent healing. Spirit healing is here to stay. It will not be dislodged. You can contribute your quota, a very important quota it is too. Always remember that you are a divine channel helping the Great Spirit in the infinite plan of evolution. It is a wonderful work that you have to do, but it is a great responsibility.

And here is the session for the Spiritualist Association of Great Britain:

"You all have knowledge of spiritual realities and so there is no need for me to impress upon you their vital importance, especially in the world today. I will help you as much as I can. You may not agree with everything that I say, but true brotherhood means that we love one another even when we cannot see eye to eye with one another. Even though you are all familiar with the manifestations of the power of the spirit in diverse forms, one of your great difficulties, because you are encased in physical bodies, is to get the correct focus, to know how real is the power of the spirit when it has the appropriate channels through which to flow.

We would be failing in everything that we seek to teach if, for a single moment, we encourage any to be deflected from their duty as citizens of the world in which they live, their duty to their families or to others who are dependent on them. But this is only a part of the story-it is not the whole story. My criticism would be, if you would forgive me speaking very frankly to you, because it is only with candour that we can help one another, that you concentrate your attention far too much on your material problems and do not have enough reliance on the power of the spirit which can solve them all.

This is the criticism that I would direct in all sincerity and humility to those of you who are, not servants of the spirit, because we are not masters, but co-operators with the spirit and who would desire to become, to the fullest possible extent, its earthly ambassadors. It is wrong for people like yourselves with knowledge to have any worry, or to allow fear to invade your being and to effect a lodgment. With the knowledge you have you should never permit any fear, any worry, any anxiety to enter into your mental, physical or spiritual surroundings. Fear, worry and anxiety – these block the very channels which can help you.

Just as grief from mourners creates a wall around them which makes it difficult for the ones they are wanting to penetrate it, so when you allow yourselves to be – surrounded with vibrations of worry you disturb the mental and spiritual atmosphere and make it even more difficult for help to come to you. You are being guided by those who love you, not only because they are associated with you by ties of blood, of affection, of friendship, but by others who are very interested in the work that you are doing because they trod this path before you. And behind them there is an even greater army of liberated souls whose only desire is to help you to serve those who come to you.

There is no limit to the power of the spirit, with all its beauty, its richness, its grandeur, its dignity, its lustre, its nobility, its radiance – except the limits you impose by the conditions that you create. Give us free channels with faith – not faith born of credulity but founded on knowledge of what you have received, the faith that you must have because it is impossible for infinite knowledge to be at your disposal at this stage of your evolution.

Rest your faith on the foundation of your knowledge. Each one of you has been led by the power of the spirit through suffering, through crises, through difficulties, to where you are now. You can look back and see how the finger of guidance has pointed the way. Have faith that, because of what has happened in the past, the power of the spirit cannot fail you, even though too often the human channel can fail the power of the spirit. We have all been richly blessed by having the sublime revelation of the reality of spiritual truths. Let us therefore show that we are worthy of the responsibilities that are entrusted to us because of the knowledge that we have gained.

The past is gone. Whatever mistakes you have made you must forget. You come into your world to make mistakes, and to learn from them. Forget the past. It is the present that matters. Serve all you can in whatever form your service can take. Do what you regard as reasonable for your material provision. Don't concern yourself overmuch about the future. Do your part and we will do ours and I can promise you that in such a co-operation there will be no failure.

You cannot measure the work that is being done in this building, which to us is hallowed and sacred ground. Here love comes into its own, tears of sorrow are dried and replaced by the smiling confidence of certainty. The sick receive alleviation and many perplexed and troubled souls find the balm of inner tranquillity as a result of direction and guidance. You cannot calculate what is being done, for you have no yardstick with which to measure the results on the soul."

Can you define the part played by spirit guidance and what should be our own efforts?

We have to work within certain laws. There are some things we can do and some things we cannot do. We are subject to laws in an even far more vigorous manner than you are. My greatest difficulty has been when I have watched those I love in the midst of crises and knew that I had to stand back, do nothing, leave them to their own devices, to see which way they choose. Often we have to say to those we love: "At this stage you are on your own. See how you fare. On your choice depends your evolution and attainment."

We are concerned with the spiritual results. You, too, often, if you will forgive me saying this, are looking at the material results. With your own Association, if you look back through history, you will find that spirit guidance has not done so badly.

We can enunciate only certain fundamental principles that are true because they are based on eternal reality. The power of the spirit cannot fail. If the earth ceased to rotate on its axis, if the tides did not move according to a preordained plan, if all the galaxies did not behave according to their pattern, then I would not be so sure. Because the Great Spirit is all-powerful and spirit is the divine power, I am confident that those who place their full reliance on that power can never fail.

You said there were times when you had to stand back and let those you love make their choice. They had free will to go which way they liked. What happens if they throw spanners into the works?

There is free will up to a point, but it is never a free free will. It is a free will that is restricted and conditioned by certain circumstances of spiritual growth and evolution. It is not a complete, unfettered free will in which you have perfect liberty of choice.

Is there no such thing as free will?

There is a free will within certain limits – you can choose which path you take at that moment and either hinder or advance your spiritual progress.

Whilst you do that, surely you may be hindering or advancing someone else?

That is possible. But may I try to explain, if I can, that on the surface all is simple. Behind the surface there are highly complex workings because there are laws within laws, within laws, within laws. Such, however, is the perfection of the Great Spirit's wisdom that all is balanced to an extent that the operation cannot fail.

Isn't it possible that the spanner that we might throw in the works isn't important enough to have much effect on the total plan?

You can throw a spanner and injure some of the works, but you cannot throw a spanner into all the works. The damage you can do is comparatively small. Nobody in your world has the means at his or her disposal to wreck completely the will of the Great Spirit, or to do the amount of damage that could prevent the divine plan from operating.

Then all these disasters that occur on our planet are within the divine plan?

In the sense that man cannot work outside the divine plan, because there is an inexorable law of cause and effect. The overruling law maintains the limitation that is imposed on man. Let me put it quite bluntly. Your scientists cannot devise means of destruction that would completely destroy the whole of the universe. That is the limitation.

Would you say that something which appears evil from the human standpoint may not be evil at all-in fact from a higher standpoint it might be regarded as good?

To many people in your world suffering is evil, pain is unwelcome, but this is not necessarily the case. Pain is just as much a part of the divine plan as pleasure. Without pain there could be no pleasure, without darkness there could be no light, without hatred there could be no love. Action and reaction are equal and opposite. They are the two sides of the same coin. Good and evil are fundamental and comparative. You have codes of morality in your world dependent on the place where you live. But it is not the same code of morality in every place. Our evaluation is based upon the effect on the soul. This is the important thing, anything which advances soul-attainment is good; anything which retards soul-attainment is bad.

I am not very happy about what you said on equal opportunities. While the spiritual essence in a soul may be the same, the instruments through which that essence will be expressed are not of equal efficiency. We cannot all gain benefit through equal opportunities. Either the opportunities presented to us vary according to our talents, or the opportunities are equal, but we are not fairly endowed so that we all have a reasonable chance of making use of them.

No, I'm sorry I cannot agree. Every human being who incarnates into the world of matter has a seed of divinity, otherwise he could not incarnate. Life is spirit and spirit is life. You have the seed of the spirit which is intended to flower. Its flowering depends upon the conditions it receives and which will affect its growth. There are equal opportunities for all human beings to develop their spiritual natures. I did not say they would attain equality of spiritual status. I said the opportunities were there. It does not matter if you are rich or poor, the service you give is not dependent upon the physical knowledge that you have.

But what about the physical abilities through which spiritual qualities are expressed?

Do you mean a child who is deformed and the brain is damaged? That is another complication with which I will deal and it involves karma.

If there is karma, is there reincarnation?
There is reincarnation, but not in the sense in which it is generally expounded. There is in our world a spiritual diamond which has many many facets. These come into your world to gain experience and to add their quota to the diamond's lustre and brilliance. Thus the personalities that are incarnated are facets of the one individuality. There is no problem really. People get confused and say, "I was So-andSo last time and I will be somebody else next time." That doesn't matter. It is the facet which has its quota to contribute to the entirety of the diamond-in that sense there is reincarnation. What you express on earth is but an infinitesimal fraction of the individuality to which you belong. Thus there are what you call "group souls," a single unity with facets which have spiritual relationships that incarnate at different times, at different places, for the purpose of equipping the larger soul for its work.

Would it be that the individuality is part of the personality, or is it the other way round?
It is the personality that is the fragment of the individuality.

If we all belong to group souls then we enjoy the experiences of others and also suffer the consequences.
Yes, it is a wise experience because we all realise that we can contribute to the whole.

So what I suffer now is not necessarily my own fault?
If that brings you consolation you are welcome to the thought. I will let you into a secret. The more knowledge you have the less choice you have. Increasing knowledge unerringly dictates the part that you must play. Those of us who have volunteered to serve must serve until our missions are accomplished. You have chosen, therefore you have no choice. Knowledge can only come when you are ready to receive it. That is how the law works. I was asked to perform a mission and I undertook to do so. The fact that you have invited me to come and talk with you shows that to some extent I may have succeeded in relaying the wisdom of others whose mouthpiece it is my privilege to be. There is a spiritual relationship that endures when the physical relationship has ended. The spiritual relationship is eternal. What binds is not matter but spirit. Matter is ephemeral, spirit is eternal.

We must gird up our loins and continue the task to which we are dedicated, bringing more and more into the orbit of the love of the Great Spirit. We must help the souls who come our way to forge those magnetic links with the spirit that will bind them forever, and enable them to be the recipients of this divine power which, when it burgeons, brings untold blessings. This is part of the task on which we are all engaged. Never let us forget the principles, the fundamentals, for when we strive to ensure that these are attained then we are fulfilling the purpose of our being.
SILVER BIRCH

Chapter Thirteen

SILVER BIRCH SUMS UP

I am conscious of my limitations and yet I know my strength and my powers. I am filled with humility, real humility, because of myself I am nothing, merely an instrument of those who sent me back to your world to perform a task, those who have endowed me with all the force and inspiration, with all the power that is at my disposal.

Myself, I am nothing, but when I represent, as I do, the mighty host of the spirit, then I can speak with certainty. Then I am repeating what they tell me to say, and they are the beings of might and majesty, the great shining ones, the evolved, the truly high in spiritual stature who strive to guide the whole of humanity.

I would be failing in my task if I did not speak to you of what I know. I am not so evolved as to be out of touch with what you call the rank and file. I know all your problems. I have lived in your world for a long time now. I have lived close to each one of you and have entered into all your difficulties. I can look back and see that never once was there anything insuperable.

Have no fear, the power of the spirit cannot work miracles because miracles do not exist. The power of the spirit can work wonders in your world provided you supply the necessary conditions. We are not on your earth. We are in a world of spirit and you have to supply us with the means by which we accomplish our work in your world.

You are our hands, you are our bodies. You provide us with the implements – and we can do the work.

We are shown how far we can go, where we must not obtrude ourselves, when we must keep silent and when we must talk. There is a definite pattern and all guides must work within that pattern because they have promised to do so. I cannot go outside the limits which have been laid down by beings far wiser than I, for it is they who have decided or planned what is to be achieved in your world.

You can call them what name you like. They are the evolved beings who are responsible for all the work that we do. They are the ones whom I have the supreme joy of meeting from time to time. I report on what I have done and am told how far I have succeeded and failed, and learn what is still expected of me.

There is another hierarchy beyond them, and beyond them too. The chain is infinite. Our world is very highly organised, far more than ever you thought was possible. To perform this task requires a miniature organisation.

We desire to help humanity, to teach it certain truths, so that it can avoid the mistakes that we and others have made on earth, learn from our wisdom, begin to utilise their divine powers, so that your world can be better, freer, richer and ours not troubled with the large number of misfits, unprepared, unequipped, unready souls who come here.

I insist that all who co-operate with us should never surrender their reason, their judgment or their free will.

Ours is a co-operation. We do not seek powers of dictatorship, we do not wish to treat you as automatons. We desire that the hand of fellowship should be clasped even across the gulf of death. Together we should labour in the common purpose of spreading knowledge that will bring freedom of body, mind and spirit to millions who know it not.

If you find that any spirit teacher, however exalted, however evolved, however learned, asks you to do that which is foreign to your nature, which seems unreasonable or unjust, then reject it. Yours is the free will and yours the personal responsibility of what you make of your own lives. We cannot live your lives for you. We can help you, we can guide you and sustain you, but we cannot transfer your responsibilities to our shoulders.

Some volunteer because they are aware of tasks to be performed in your world. Others who have reached a maturity of spiritual growth are approached by those who have taken upon themselves the task of helping humanity. I was asked – I did not choose in the first place. But when I was asked whether I would volunteer to do so, I readily assented.

I can tell you that a very black picture was painted of the difficulties that would have to be surmounted before any progress could be made. Yet, to a large extent, those difficulties have been conquered. The obstacles that still stand in the way are very small compared with those that have been removed.

We desire that you should live the fullest life, the life in which all talents and faculties and gifts find their fullest manifestation. Thus you will serve the purpose of your earthly being and will be ready for the next stage of life when the door of death opens to you.

That is the standard which I lay down. I think I can say without contradiction of my friends who have known me for a long time that I enthrone reason as the supreme arbiter.

In our world, what you are determines what you do. It is your spirit that is the dominant reality. There are no masks, no disguises, no subterfuges, no cheats. There is nothing hidden; all is known.

I never accept thanks. Thanks should be rendered to the Great Spirit, whose servants we all are. I strive to perform this task. I do it with willingness and cheerfulness. If anything I have said has been of help, then it is because I am going about my Father's business.

You have never seen me. You do not know me except as a voice speaking to you through this body. But let me assure you that I am a very real person with the ability to feel, to know and to love.

This is the real world, not yours. You will not understand the reality until you have left your earthly planet.

Let us thank the Great Spirit for this opportunity given to us to disperse the obstacles between the two planes of being. Let us rejoice that we can commune with one another, spirit to spirit, heart to heart, mind to mind, across the gulf of what is called death. Let us always strive to render the greatest service we can wherever we can, to refuse none who ask our help, to bring any comfort to those in trouble, so that it has always been worth their while to come into our orbit.

Let us recognise that we are the emissaries of the mightiest force in the universe, the Great Spirit of all life. And let us discharge the duties that are laid upon us in such a fashion that we will qualify for that inner peace that comes to all those who strive to be at one with the power that endowed them with the gift of life itself.

SILVER BIRCH

Chapter Fourteen

SELECTED SILVER BIRCH SAYINGS

Sowing and reaping are part of the natural law which I wish was accepted by more people. It is in the cultivation of the fruits of the earth that you learn how inexorable are the laws of the Great Spirit. He who lives close to the soil and sees the operation of nature's law begins to appreciate the divine handiwork, and realise something of the Mind which has planned all in its orderly sequence.

That which is garnered is that which has been sown. The seed is always true to type. You cannot sow the seed of a potato and expect that a lettuce will grow. Always what has been sown will follow unswervingly the dictate of the natural law. And what is true in that realm of nature is equally true in the realm of human life and activity.

We cannot change your world overnight. There is no equivalent of the trumpet blast that will destroy the walls of today's materialistic Jericho. We have to proceed slowly by evolutionary, not revolutionary, methods, reaching one at a time. We do not want any attempts at emotional mass conversions that dissipate in the cold light of morning.

We want souls to come into their own through selfrealisation because they are convinced and know, not through knowledge obtained necessarily in books, but through the infallible knowledge that comes from within when you have strengthened the link that binds you to the Great Spirit and realise that you are part of an endless spiritual chain.

If saintliness could be achieved without difficulty, it would not have any value. If those who sin could, by the recital of some words, banish the consequence of their selfishness, divine justice would become a mockery and certainly worse than its human counterpart.

Spiritual attainment is a long, slow, difficult path. As the pilgrim embarks on it, he leaves behind many familiar landscapes and journeys more and more into the unknown. But, as compensation, which is part of the natural law, he begins to have the warmth and beauty, the nobility and lustre, the grandeur and divinity of the spirit as part of his natural accompaniment. This is the law of compensation in action.

*   *   *

Nature, which is a reflection of the Great Spirit's handiwork, cannot be hastened, neither can the unfoldment of life as expressed through physical bodies. There must be a balance in order to have harmony. What you will get, as time goes on, is an increasing process of attunement, a growing awareness of the presence of those who are linked with you in the task you are performing.

This depends on your own spiritual growth, so that you can achieve a merging and fusion of your being with others in our world. It is hard to explain because it is a spiritual process, not a physical one. The attributes of the spirit have to be expressed and unfold slowly, naturally and in orderly fashion. As they do so, increasing awareness comes.

My appeal is always to reason and common sense. If I say anything that makes your reason revolt or insults your intelligence, discard it. You should not accept any utterance from your world or mine that does not appeal to you. I cannot make plain to you matters of spiritual import that require an understanding of conditions beyond earth in order to be more fully appreciated.

I have never witnessed anything that is not in accordance with divine law, divine love, divine wisdom and divine justice. As progress is eternal you cannot see the whole picture. You have some knowledge and on that base you must build a faith that is reasonable, not one that is incredulous.

*　　*　　*

You cannot have instant mediumship. Your world is always anxious for short cuts to everything. But there are no short cuts to spiritual attainment. Soul growth is necessarily slow, but it is sure. The soul cannot grow and achieve its next stage of development until it is ready to do so.

You are on the right road, which is all that matters. Allegiance to truth wins through in the end. No matter how hostile the enemy, vigorous the opposition or tenacious the vested interest, truth breaks through. The battle is slowly but surely being won. It is not A uniform progress, but once the battle is won it can never be lost, or have to be fought again.

You are concerned with healing because this gift has been developed in you. Your responsibility is to be as pure an instrument as you can for the power of the spirit to flow through you. You are not responsible for what the patient does. You cannot say whether or not you will achieve success, either with his body, mind, or in touching his soul. This is outside your province. You offer yourself in service and those who use you will do the best they can to help the ones who are brought to you for healing.

Do not worry about what happens to patients. That is their responsibility. They have their supreme chance when they cross your threshold. Serve them is all that you are asked to do. You cannot lift the burden from everybody's shoulders. It is their burden, they have placed it there and they must remove it. This is not said in any spirit of asperity or harshness, but to state a literal truth.

*   *   *

As our teaching grows in your world, it will mean the end of separateness between peoples. It will mean the end of national barriers, race distinctions, class distinctions, colour distinctions and all the distinctions between churches and chapels, temples, mosques and synagogues. All will learn they have a part to play in the Great Spirit's truth and that the part enshrined in the heart of every other religion in no way contradicts that portion which is precious to them.

So, out of apparent confusion, the divine pattern will take shape, and harmony and peace will come. What we teach fits in with all the noble and elevated ideas that have come to the visions of reformers, saints, seers and idealists who have striven in every age to render service.

The secret of life is to be found in the proper exercise of the spirit, mind and body. It is wrong to dwell only on the spirit and ignore the responsibilities of the body. It is equally wrong and foolish to concentrate on the body and ignore the responsibilities of the spirit. You must learn to establish concert, rhythm, harmony, balance and wholeness. Then you are at peace with the Great Spirit, with the world and with everybody in it and, most important of all, with yourself.

This is because you are fulfilling yourself. You are allowing the Great Spirit to manifest in your life. What you need will be supplied. The incorruptible, untarnishable, jewels of the spirit once gained can never dwindle or be lost.

*   *   *

Man and woman are complementary to one another. Each has qualities the other lacks. When there is perfect harmony, when two halves make one whole, there, indeed is the fulness of the great plan expressed. In too many cases the coming together of two souls on earth does not achieve this fulness. The union is not actuated by that great power which alone is capable of uniting two souls in one eternal bond.

Love is the greatest force. Love works wonders that no other power can achieve. Love desires no ill for its beloved or anybody else. The true marriage, the enduring marriage, is when two souls are in harmony.

We receive, day after day, the misfits, the derelicts, the outcasts, the flotsam and jetsam, the millions who come here unprepared, unready, unequipped and who have to learn all over again. Instead of passing to our world a stream of evolved souls ready to take up the tasks that await them, there come millions who have to be treated and nursed and tended because they are like bruised little children.

This is why it is so important that man should receive truth, for with truth to guide him he cannot fail. Truth will bring understanding, peace and love. With love in his heart there is no problem that cannot be solved. All the problems confronting the leaders of mankind today would fade away if truth, wisdom, knowledge and love were to rule and guide humanity.

*　*　*

There is no new truth. Truth is truth. There is knowledge which depends upon the individual being ready to receive it. When you are children you are taught according to your capacity to assimilate. You begin with the letters of your alphabet and, as the mind grows, you are taught to make words and read. Gradually the knowledge contained in the printed word becomes accessible to you.

The knowledge you receive is dependent upon your capacity for appreciating it. There is an infinity of wisdom which can become available only as you are mentally and spiritually equipped to receive it. But no knowledge alters truth, which is constant and eternal. You can add to wisdom, to knowledge, but you cannot bring new truth.

COMPLETE YOUR COLLECTION

All of Silver Birch's books make superb reading, providing inspiration, illumination and perhaps occasionally consolation. Over the years, the guide answered literally thousands of questions on almost every subject imaginable. The complete list of available Silver Birch titles is shown below. These can be read and enjoyed either individually or as a complete set, one which makes a unique collection to refer to time and time again. Each volume gives the guide's views on a comprehensive range of topics both here and hereafter.

The Silver Birch Book of Questions and Answers
Compiled by Stan A. Ballard and Roger Green. This latest Silver Birch title is in easy-to-read question-and-answer form. It answers literally hundreds of points, such as. "Do we reincarnate on earth?", "What are the spiritual aspects of heart transplant surgery?" and "Can euthanasia ever be right?"   240 pages £8.50

The Seed of Truth
Compiled by Tony Ortzen. Based upon two earlier out-of-print titles *Silver Birch Speaks* and *More Wisdom of Silver Birch* which were compiled by the medium's wife, Sylvia. It contains an account of when actress Mary Pickford, "the world's sweetheart," met and questioned Silver Birch. Each chapter ends with one of the guide's uplifting prayers.
                      174 pages £8.50

Lift Up Your Hearts
Compiled by Tony Ortzen. This carefully chosen selection of teaching comprises the guide's wise words over a twenty-year period. Animals, a spirit view of death, mediumship and karma are just four of the many subjects explained. Features a verbatim account of when Doris Stokes and Doris Collins, two of Britain's most famous mediums, were addressed by Silver Birch.   229 pages £8.50

Philosophy of Silver Birch
Edited by Stella Storm. A former secretary to Maurice Barbanell and then chief reporter at *Psychic News*, Stella Storm covers such issues as natural law, lessons of bereavement, the responsibility of mediumship and "Healing, the greatest gift of all." Silver Birch also tells what he would say to a television audience. This popular book is now in its sixth impression. 155 pages £8.50

More Philosophy of Silver Birch
Compiled by Tony Ortzen. In easy to read question-and-answer form, of special interest are two chapters which trace man from birth to what lies Beyond. Social problems, reincarnation and science are amongst other subjects examined. This title ends with inspiring bite-sized "points to ponder."   253 pages £8.50

Silver Birch Companion
Edited by Tony Ortzen. Drawing upon *More Teachings of Silver Birch* and *Wisdom of Silver Birch*, this volume features an account of the night Maurice Barbanell died and the days that followed. Features the replies the guide gave to a Fleet Street editor.   159 pages £8.50

A Voice in the Wilderness
Edited by Tony Ortzen. Most of the material in this book came from handpicked cuttings at the archives of *Psychic News*, though it also draws upon the out-of-print *Home Circle* and *Spirit Guidance*. Read the advice the guide gave to a Member of Parliament, a senior Army chaplain and delegates at an International Spiritualist Federation congress.   128 pages £6.00

The Spirit Speaks
Compiled by Tony Ortzen. An abridged amalgamation not only of *Silver Birch Speaks Again* and *Anthology of Silver Birch* but also important teachings that originally appeared in *Psychic News*. Amongst its highlights is a word-for-word report of a meeting betwen Silver Birch and film star Merle Oberon, who was devastated when her fiancé was killed in a plane crash.   142 pages £8.50

Guidance from Silver Birch
Edited by Anne Dooley. A former Fleet Street journalist, Anne Dooley later became a reporter at *Psychic News*, first 'meeting' Silver Birch in 1963. Amongst subjects in this compilation are the problems of suffering and communication with the spirit world.   120 pages £6.00

Teachings of Silver Birch
Edited by A.W.Austen. First published in 1938, this classic Silver Birch title has so far run to seven impressions. It contains a fascinating Foreword by famous journalist Hannen Swaffer, after whom the Silver Birch circle was named. Silver Birch tells his own story and, as usual, answers countless questions, including life in the spirit realms.   243 pages £8.50

Silver Birch Anthology
Edited by William Naylor. Love's supreme power, what happens after we die and "Who is Silver Birch?" are just three of the topics in this absorbing book. Originally published in 1955, the philosophy within this book is still fresh, vital and valuable.   132 pages £6.00

Light from Silver Birch
Compiled by Pam Riva. Contains the last ever teachings from Silver Birch after the sudden passing of his medium Maurice Barbanell on July 17th, 1981. Also featured is Maurice Barbanell's obituary, which, ever the keen journalist, he prepared in advance. His mission with Silver Birch lasted sixty-one years. Pam Riva was the medium's secretary at *Psychic News*, the paper he founded in 1932.
                    218 pages £8.50

The Universe of Silver Birch
By Frank Newman. This book is unique as Frank Newman has examined Silver Birch's teachings and measured them side by side with the deductions of modern science. This brings important new insights into Silver Birch's philosophy. The result is an intriguing, thought-provoking volume.   118 pages £8.50

· · · · · ·

Silver Birch Speaks   Now you can hear the guide in the comfort of your own home. This sixty-minute cassette was recorded at a special sitting, during which a selection of questions was put to the guide.

Silver Birch Meditation Print After Silver Birch was painted by psychic artist Marcel Poncin, the oil portrait had pride of place in Maurice Barbanell's London flat. Now it is available as a full colour A5-size card. The reverse contains an inspiring message from Silver Birch.

How to order:

Please post or telephone your order to
STF Publications, New Barn, Runnington,
Wellington TA21 0QJ.
Telephone 01823 665338.
The cost of postage and packing will be
advised upon receipt of order.

Credit card payments can be made via PayPal.

Please make cheques or postal orders payable to

STF Publications Ltd.

Only sterling cheques can be accepted.
Telephone 01823 665338.

The cost of postage and packing will be
advised upon receipt of order.

Credit card payments can be made via PayPal.

Please make cheques or postal orders payable to
STF Publications Ltd.

Only sterling cheques can be accepted.